# CLARKE'S MEADOW & THE CALYPSO KINGS

Dave Bracegirdle

REID PUBLISHING

A CIP catalogue record for this title is available from the British Library

ISBN: 978-0-9558807-6-6

Book Design by Andrew Searle

Published by Reid Publishing
53 Church Gate, Loughborough,
Leicestershire, LE11 1UE
Tel: 07974 304022  Email: reidpublishing@fsmail.net

Printed and bound by CPI Group (UK) Ltd, Croydon, CR0 4YY

# CONTENTS

# ACKNOWLEDGEMENTS

A huge debt of thanks is due to several wonderful people who have helped in the creation and publication of '*Clarke's Meadow & The Calypso Kings*'.

Many of them can't be named, as some of the information has stemmed from uncredited reports that have been provided by various contributors to Wisden Cricketers' Almanack, Notts CCC Year Books, assorted cricket annuals, internet sites, books, brochures and scorecards.

More specifically, I must thank Michael Temple, Nottinghamshire's Head of Marketing & Communications, plus Chris Botherway, New Media Manager. Both have freely given of their time and expertise to source information and photographs for me.

Other photographs in this book have kindly been supplied by the Portrait Collective and the Nottingham Post, with special thanks going to Carolyn Maginnis for her accuracy and patience in identifying suitable images.

The real graft in putting it all together has been done by Andrew Searle, who, together with David McVay, have been pivotal in getting this project off the ground – many thanks to you both gentlemen.

Finally my appreciation goes to the numerous players, officials and supporters who have either been interviewed, offered advice or been a source of inspiration, to John Ellison for his assistance in marketing the book and to Karen for her devoted support.

Dave Bracegirdle
March 2012

# INTRODUCTION

The West Indian cricket team were hailed as the most formidable on the planet as they swept all before them from the mid 1970s until the early 1990s. A battery of fearsome fast bowlers, an array of attacking stroke-makers, plus the ruthlessly efficient captaincy of Clive Lloyd initially, and then Vivian Richards later, ensured almost total dominance throughout the period.

For much longer than that though, the West Indies have found a little 'home away from home' whenever they have visited Nottingham and played their cricket at Trent Bridge. In 1900 a touring side, playing a series of friendly matches, lost to Notts but since then no West Indian side has ever lost a first class match at Trent Bridge.

On 22 occasions – fourteen of them in first class fixtures against Notts and the other eight being Test Matches against England – the West Indies have remained unbeatable on the ground that was formerly an old meadow at the back of The Trent Bridge Inn, where William Clarke lived after marrying landlady Mary Chapman.

*'Clarke's Meadow and the Calypso Kings'* tells the story of some of the greatest cricketers ever to leave the Caribbean and records the outcome of their appearances in Nottingham. From Harold Austin, captain of the first touring side more than a century ago, right through to the greats of the modern era, all of the true West Indian legends have made their mark.

Early stars were George Challenor, who scored hundreds on both occasions he played against Notts, the hostile quick bowler Manny Martindale and the majestic George Headley – whose batting earned him the nickname of 'The Black Bradman'.

During the fifties, the three Ws – Everton Weekes, Frank Worrell and Clyde Walcott – all made the most of the batsman-friendly Trent Bridge square, whilst the mercurial spin twins Valentine and Ramadhin bamboozled England's batsmen with their wily skills.

The sixties brought the world's number one player, Garfield Sobers, backed up by such luminaries as Basil Butcher, Wes Hall and Charlie Griffith.

The kindness of the fixture schedulers presented Trent Bridge with the opening Test match of the 1976 summer. However glorious the weather, the controversial pre-match comments from England captain Tony Greig increased the atmosphere to white-hot, with the eyes of the world looking on.

Roberts, Holding, Garner, Bishop, Daniel, Marshall, Ambrose and Walsh have all come off the Caribbean conveyor belt of fast bowlers during the last thirty years and shone in Nottingham, whilst on the batting front the likes of Lara, Gayle and Chanderpaul have carried on the tradition of their illustrious countrymen by turning in outstanding performances when they have toured.

Pitting their talents against such luminaries has always presented county players with a great opportunity to impress and over the years several Notts players have risen to the occasion in outstanding fashion. Wilfred Payton, John Gunn, Arthur Carr, Reg Simpson, Mike Harris and Mike Smedley – twice – all scored hundreds against the Test nation, whilst their presence in this country also saw Paul Franks make his England One Day International debut on his home ground in 2000.

Nottinghamshire's relationship with West Indian cricketers doesn't just extend to them being welcomed on infrequent tours, of course. Going back to Carlton Forbes, in the late fifties, on through the likes of Deryck Murray, Franklyn Stephenson, Vasbert Drakes and Jimmy Adams amongst others, the county side has welcomed and embraced all of their calypso cricketers.

Missing from that list is one name that will forever be associated with the county. When Garfield Sobers joined Notts in 1968, it was a ground-breaking move, engineered to raise the profile of the club. Sobers – now, of course, Sir Garfield Sobers – was already a record-breaker when he came to Trent Bridge, having held the highest individual Test match score of 365 not out since 1958. In his first season with Notts he also became the first cricketer to score six sixes in an over when he hit Glamorgan's Malcolm Nash for 36 from one over.

The left hander maintains a wonderful relationship with Trent Bridge, and with the Notts supporters, who were able to embrace a new West Indian star in Darren Bravo towards the latter part of the 2011 season. Bravo's brief time on the Trent Bridge staff – plus an account of Nottinghamshire's first official tour of Barbados - brings up a fitting conclusion to this book, released ahead of West Indies' 2012 tour of the UK.

# The Early Days

# 1900

The first cricket side to represent the entire West Indies region made a tour of the British Isles during the summer of 1900. Several of the leading players were unavailable to tour and the MCC ruled that none of the seventeen arranged fixtures would be afforded first class status.

Aucher Warner of Trinidad was the official tour captain, but malarial fever restricted him to just seven appearances. It was clearly a tour to forget for him as he lost the toss in all seven of the matches that he did play in. His deputy was Stanley Sproston of British Guiana.

Heavy defeats were a feature of the opening few fixtures. By the time of their arrival at Nottingham in July the West Indians had lost five of the seven matches, with their only victories coming against the Minor Counties and Leicestershire.

At Trent Bridge the young tour side were soon up against it. As usual Warner had lost the toss and seen the opposition run up a score of 501, with William Gunn scoring 161 in 210 minutes out of 274. At the close of the opening day, the county side had made 343-4 and were then indebted to 101 from James Iremonger to boost them to their final total.

Tommy Burton, a Barbados-born medium-pacer, worked his way to figures of 5-159 from a mammoth 73.3 overs.

The West Indies reached 124-6 by stumps, with Percy Cox – who began his career with Barbados before switching to Trinidad – reaching 55.

On the final day Warner reached 53 not out, but his side were forced to follow on and were dismissed again to lose by an innings and 27 runs.

This would be the only time in the 20th century that Nottinghamshire would taste success over the West Indians, although the match was not first class.

*9, 10, 11 July 1900*
*Notts 501 (W Gunn 161, Iremonger 101, Burton 5-159)*
*West Indians 209 (Cox 55, A Warner 53\*) and 265 (Sproston 72,*
*Olivierre 50, Constantine 50\*)*
*Notts won by an innings and 27 runs*

The tour was considered a great success, despite only five of the seventeen matches being won. Burton was the leading wicket-taker, with 78 from the 16 matches he played in.

Charles Olivierre of St Vincent had scored a half century in the second innings of the defeat at Trent Bridge. He accumulated 883 runs during the tour, playing in all 17 matches and top scoring with 159 against Leicestershire at an average of 32.70. Olivierre returned to the UK in 1901 to begin a seven year stint with Derbyshire.

# 1906 TO 1950

Captained by Harold Austin from Barbados, the first West Indian side to undertake a first class tour of the British Isles was made in 1906. The tourists played thirteen matches, all of them scheduled to last for three days.

Alien conditions certainly counted against them early on, as the opening seven matches were decisively lost, five of them to county sides and one to a WG Grace XI, with 'the good doctor' helping himself to eight wickets in the match. In what was seen as the showpiece match of the tour, they also went down by six wickets at Lord's to an MCC side whose own skipper, Pelham Warner, had himself been born in Port-of-Spain, Trinidad, and had been part of the side that had toured here six years earlier.

Performances and results picked up after that. Of the remaining seven fixtures, only one was lost, whilst there were three victories (over Scotland, Yorkshire and Northants), plus two draws – including the game at Trent Bridge. Beginning on 13 August 1906, Nottinghamshire made 254-5 on a rain-interrupted opening day. Having elected to bat first, the county side were indebted to Stapleford-born Wilfred Payton, who made 113, his maiden century.

The West Indian side included wicketkeeper-batsman Lebrun Constantine, father of Learie, who would later make 18 Test appearances, but neither he, nor his team-mates, fared well with the bat as Wass and Hallam took nine wickets between them on the second day, skittling the West Indian XI for 149 in response to 296.

Second time around Notts could only reach 180, thanks largely to John Gunn's 112, meaning the tourists were set a victory target of 328. George Challenor, an 18-year-old opening batsman from Barbados who had only played in two first class matches before being selected for the tour, made 108 – his maiden first class century – as the game finished in a draw with his side closing on 292-7

Twenty-two years later, in June 1928, Challenor,  a week before his fortieth birthday, played in the West Indies' very first Test match (against England at Lord's) and was dismissed by Nottinghamshire's Harold Larwood.

*13, 14, 15 August 1906*
*Nottinghamshire 296 (Payton 113) and 180 (J Gunn 112)*
*West Indians 149 and 292-7 (Challenor 108)*
*Match Drawn*

# 1923

Despite the MCC sending tour parties to the Caribbean in 1910-11 and 1912-13, a return visit to these shores wasn't made until 1923. Between the end of May and the beginning of September that summer, the tourists played a total of 20 first class matches, including the fixture in Nottingham in July.

There were a couple of familiar faces in the tour party. Harold Austin was again skipper, although he was plagued by illness for much of the summer and only played in eleven of the matches, and George Challenor also returned.

Although the contest against Nottinghamshire was again drawn, there were some outstanding individual performances in a high-scoring match. Notts made 353, with half-centuries for Wilfred Payton, George Gunn, Robert Turner and Lionel Kirk, with the opposition coming back with a creditable 317.

Joe Small, from Trinidad and Tobago, enjoyed a fine all-round match, top-scoring with 71 after taking five wickets in the Notts innings. Challenor and Dewhurst also passed fifty. Cyril Browne – known to one and all as Snuffy Browne – collected figures of 7-97 with his right-arm medium-paced bowling, to restrict Notts to a second innings score of 345 – with Kirk's 86 leading the way.

Echoing the previous tour, the West Indians gave a spirited showing in their second innings, as both openers went on to score unbeaten centuries. Challenor, getting good runs at Trent Bridge for the second time in his career, ended on 102, whilst his partner Percy Tarilton finished on 109, with the stand worth 219 in pursuit of 382.

*4, 5, 6 July 1923*
*Notts 353 (Payton 84, Small 5-93) and 345*
*(Kirk 86, Browne 7-97)*
*West Indians 317 (Small 71) and 219-0*
*(Tarilton 109\*, Challenor 102 \*)*
*Match Drawn*

# 1928

The 1928 tour of the British Isles was undoubtedly the most important made by the West Indians to that point, as it enabled them to join England, Australia and South Africa as the fourth Test playing nation. In truth, their elevation to the highest level of the game didn't go well, with them losing all three Test matches to England by some distance.

The make up of the West Indian side for their first ever Test is interesting, with four Trinidad and Tobago players (Wilton St Hill, Cliff Roach, Learie Constantine and Joe Small), four from Barbados (George Challenor, Snuffy Browne, George Francis and Herman Griffith, who had been born in Trinidad but played all of his cricket for Barbados), captain Karl Nunes and Frank Martin came from Jamaica, whilst Maurice Fernandes was the lone Guyanese representative.

Between the first couple of Test matches the West Indians travelled around the country, squeezing in six matches against county sides. The fourth of those matches was in Nottingham, in early July. Nunes skippered a side that featured eight of those that had been on duty at Lord's, although Challenor was rested, thereby missing the opportunity of being able to score a Trent Bridge hundred for the third tour running.

There were a couple of centurions, although the fixture again ended in a draw. Arthur Carr, captaining Nottinghamshire, made exactly 100 out of his side's first day total of 393 all out. Edward 'Barto' Bartlett, a right-handed batsman from Barbados – who would eventually get his chance in the Test side at the Kennington Oval later in the summer – made 109 out of 378, before becoming one of Harold Larwood's three victims. Sam Staples took the bowling honours for the county side, claiming 5-99 with his off-breaks.

With time running out in the match, Notts declared on 246-6 second time around, leaving their visitors to close on 85 without loss, chasing a nominal 262.

*7, 9, 10 July 1928*
*Notts 393 (Carr 100) and 246-6 dec*
*West Indians 378 (Bartlett 109, Staples 5-99) and 85-0*
*Match Drawn*

# 1933

By the time of the next West Indian cricket tour to the British Isles, they had been able to celebrate a couple of Test victories of their own, one at home to an under-strength England, who also had a side out in New Zealand at the same time, and one in Australia, although that series was won 4-1 by the hosts.

There was plenty of controversy at the start of that tour, with the hosts putting the seven white members of the West Indian party in one Sydney hotel, with the other eleven black members of the squad put in another. Understandably, complaints were made and the Australian Board successfully persuaded their Government to remove this blatant discrimination

The 1933 English summer began in the aftermath of more controversy, arriving straight after the Bodyline series down under. Again here for the full season, the West Indians had a 30-match programme of fixtures to play, including three Tests.

Although Trent Bridge had been used as a Test match venue since 1899, it still wasn't given one of the West Indies matches, with these scheduled for Lord's, Old Trafford and the Kennington Oval. Nottingham again had to make do with just a county match in early July.

Despite it being the height of the summer season, rain intervened to leave the match drawn – the fourth straight occasion when the fixture had failed to provide a positive outcome. The contest did, however, provide one outstanding individual performance to reflect upon.

Fast bowler Manny Martindale, from Barbados, had been creating quite an impression as he made his way around the circuit. Playing against Essex, at the County Ground, Leyton, he had been too hot to handle and collected figures of 8-32 from 15.3 overs. His early season form had impressed sufficiently for the selectors to award him his international debut in the opening Test of the summer and he picked up four England wickets, beginning with that of Herbert Sutcliffe.

High on confidence, he maintained his form at Nottingham in devastating fashion. George Headley's 66 had helped the visitors to 314 on the first day. Rain showers then frequently disrupted the reply, although they became more preferable than facing the pacy Martindale, who ended with figures of 29.2-9-66-8.

During the Second Test match, at Old Trafford, the West Indian duo of Martindale and Learie Constantine tried to give England a taste of their own 'Bodyline' medicine, bowling quick, short-pitched deliveries around the wicket and aimed at the rib-cage area, but the hosts were able to withstand the onslaught as the match finished in a draw.

Astonishingly, Manny Martindale went on to take 103 first class wickets, at an average of 20.98. He played in 25 of the 30 matches and his haul included eight five-wicket or better performances.

Tour batting honours went to another Barbadian, George Headley. In 23 matches he scored 2320 first class runs, at 66.28, with seven centuries and a top score of 224 not out.

*8, 10, 11 July 1933*
*West Indians 314 (Headley 66) and 6-0*
*Notts 273 (Walker 70, Martindale 8-66))*
*Match Drawn*

# 1939

With Europe on the brink of war, the West Indies' 1939 tour was cut short and the players returned home straight after the drawn third Test match, leaving England 1-0 series winners. Since their last tour here, the West Indies had defeated England 2-1 in the Caribbean, with George Headley's 270 not out paving the way for the historic series-clinching win at Sabina Park, Jamaica.

Headley arrived in Nottingham after scoring centuries in both innings of the Lord's Test match. Six years earlier he had looked set for a big score on his previous visit to Trent Bridge, before nicking Arthur Staples through to wicket-keeper Ben Lilley for 66. Clearly then, there was some unfinished business as far as George Headley and Nottingham were concerned and he made full use of his next opportunity to score runs there.

He arrived in the middle of the 1939 fixture with his side already in the ascendancy after dismissing Notts for just 149. Joe Hardstaff jnr had made 73 not out for the county but had received little in the way of support, principally from the middle and lower order, who were blown away by Learie Constantine's 6-50.

The West Indians lost captain Rolph Grant early on but were ahead at the close of the first day, on 169-1. Vic Stollmeyer was unbeaten on 73 but ill health forced him to retire when play resumed on the Monday morning. Gerry Gomez made 40, but then Headley established a punishing partnership with wicket-keeper Derek Sealy, which was eventually worth 230 for the third wicket.

Sealy made 115 and shortly after he had been dismissed Grant decided to declare, leaving Headley unbeaten on 234, the first instance of a West Indian batsman scoring a double hundred at Trent Bridge – but certainly not the last!

Second time around, Notts fared a little better, reaching 267, thanks largely to Walter Keeton's 82, but they were decisively beaten, with Martindale and Constantine again amongst the second innings wicket-takers.

Although he didn't make an impression – neither batting nor bowling – the West Indian side included Ken Weekes, a left-handed batsman who had been born in Boston, Massachusetts and who eventually died in Brooklyn, New York. He made two Test appearances, becoming the first player to be born in the USA to grace that stage – and the only one until 2002 when Jehan Mubarak of Sri Lanka (born Washington DC) followed him.

Ken's impact on the game was fairly minimal, but he did score four first class centuries for Jamaica in a 30-match career. His cousin Everton left a more lasting impression on the game of cricket though, and would feature quite significantly when the tourists would next appear in Nottingham.

*1, 3, 4 July 1939*
*Notts 149 (Hardstaff 73 no, Constantine 6-50)*
*and 267 (Keeton 82)*
*West Indians 510-3 dec (Headley 234 no, Sealy 115)*
*West Indians won by an Innings and 94 runs*

# Victory Calypso

# 1950

The West Indies returned to the Test match arena in 1948, defeating the MCC 2-0 in a four match series played across the Caribbean. They then embarked on trips to India, Pakistan and Ceylon, as it then was.

During this period some new and exciting talent had been unearthed, with three young Barbadians forcing their way into the side for the first time. All three had been born within 17 months of each other and within a mile of the Kensington Oval in Barbados. Later, they became universally known as 'The Three Ws' but at the time of the 1950 tour of England, Everton Weekes, Clyde Walcott and Frank Worrell were just like the rest of the party, just keen to make an impression and win a series there for the first time.

Of the three, Weekes had been quickest to show his international pedigree, emphatically proving what a high-class batsman he already was. Spread over four matches between the final home Test against England (MCC) and into the first three Tests on the Indian tour, he had become the first batsman to score centuries in five consecutive Test match innings. The sequence ended when he was run out for 90 at Madras in the Fourth Test.

John Goddard of Barbados captained the 1950 tour party, who arrived in Nottingham directly after losing the opening Test of the summer at Old Trafford. Losing that match by 202 runs was particularly hard on Alf Valentine. The 20-year-old slow left arm spinner had forced his way into the starting eleven for Manchester by taking thirteen wickets the previous week against Lancashire.

On the opening morning of the series Valentine, thrust into the attack early, took the first five England wickets before lunch and ended with eight for 104 on his international debut. He took a total of 13 wickets in the match and was well-supported by another spinner making his senior bow, 21-year-old Sonny Ramadhin.

Neither spinner was included in the match against Nottinghamshire, which was again spread between Saturday and Tuesday, with the Sunday being a rest day. The Notts bowlers, nine of whom were used, were certainly in need of that rest day, having been hit for 525-5 from the 130 overs bowled.

At 80-2, and with both openers gone, Notts would have been satisfied with their early progress, but they were then put firmly on the back foot by a stand of 163 for the third wicket. Only the run out of Frank Worrell for 83 brought a temporary halt to the onslaught.

The day belonged to Everton Weekes, however. He scored a mammoth 279. Charlie Macartney's Trent Bridge record score of 345, compiled during the Australians' 1921 tour, had appeared under threat until the tiring Weekes was bowled by Hardstaff.

During the final two days of the match the West Indians picked up the 20 wickets they needed to complete their first success on the ground. The leg breaks of Cecil Williams helped skittle Notts for 240 and, following-on, Worrell also claimed five wickets, although a defiant century from Reg Simpson delayed the inevitable.

Winning at Trent Bridge was the perfect tonic for the tourists, knowing that they would be back there soon – to play their maiden Test match in Nottingham.

*17, 19, 20 June 1950*
*West Indians 525-5 dec (Weekes 279, Worrell 83)*
*Notts 240 (Stocks 68, Williams 5-54)*
*and 224 (Simpson 109, Worrell 5-57)*
*West Indians won by an innings and 61 runs*

# THE FIFTIES

Trent Bridge's first Test match between England the West Indies took place in July 1950. It was the third match in a four-game series and began with each side having already gained a victory.

As detailed in the previous chapter, England had triumphed at Old Trafford – despite Alf Valentine's incredible debut – but at Lord's it was Trinidad and Tobago's Sonny Ramadhin who stole the show, claiming match figures of 11-152 to spin his side to a 326-run victory. Valentine took seven of the other wickets to tumble

Opener Allan Rae had scored a first innings 106 for the West Indies, but in the second knock the middle order went to work. Clyde Walcott's 168 not out, backed by Gomez (70), Weekes (63) and Worrell (45) left England chasing 601, a totally unrealistic objective, despite a century from Cyril Washbrook.

And so to Nottingham: After their humbling defeat at 'The Home of Cricket' England were forced into making changes and they did so with relish. Out went Hutton, Edrich, Doggart, Wardle and Berry, to be replaced by two debutants, Doug Insole, the Essex middle order batsman and medium pacer, plus Derek Shackleton, the Hampshire opening bowler. There were also recalls for Eric Hollies of Warwickshire, John Dewes of Middlesex and, most pleasing for the home supporters, Reg Simpson of Nottinghamshire.

Simpson had played in the opening match of the summer, at Manchester, but had missed the game at Lord's. A Trent Bridge century against the tourists for his county side must have helped his cause because he was now back for his fifth Test appearance – and his first on home soil.

As a statistical aside, the make-up of the England team meant that for the first time eleven different counties were represented.

Yorkshire's Norman Yardley won the toss for England and elected to bat first, but the decision soon backfired as they slumped to 25-4, with the new ball providing Hines Johnson and Frank Worrell, bowling his useful left arm seamers, each with a couple of wickets.

A succession of 20s, 30s and 40s from the middle order lifted England to 223, but the West Indies, despite the loss of Jeffrey Stollmeyer, already had 77 on the board by the close of the opening day.

Robert Christiani fell for 10 early the next day, providing Shackleton with his first Test wicket. Allan Rae made 68, but at 238-3 the West Indies were already ahead when Worrell and Weekes joined forces. Just a month earlier the pair had added 163 on the same ground against Nottinghamshire. This time they kept going well into the third morning, by which time they had put on 283 in 210 minutes.

Worrell was eventually dismissed for 261, a score that remains as the highest ever hit on the ground by an overseas player in Test cricket. Everton Weekes' contribution was 129, but then the tail collapsed spectacularly as the last seven wickets fell for just 37 runs, with Bedser's 48-over shift being rewarded with figures of 5-127.

Batting again, 335 behind, England needed a good start – and by golly, they got one! Washbrook and Simpson remained together for more than five hours in adding 212 for the first wicket, a record against the West Indies. Both men then fell in quick succession, Washbrook for 102 and Simpson, tragically, run out for 94.

Parkhouse, Dewes and Evans all passed fifty as England showed they had the stomach for a fight. They batted for 245.2 overs in reaching 436, with the bowling figures of the two principle spinners worth examining closely:

A Valentine 92-49-140-3
S Ramadhin 81.2-25-135-5

Needing 102 to take the lead in the series, openers Rae and Stollmeyer were still together when the total was reached in the 37th over. A ten-wicket victory was not a bad way for the West Indies to celebrate their first Test appearance at Trent Bridge and improve their already useful record on the ground.

The final Test of that 1950 summer was played at the Kennington Oval and Rae and Worrell scored first innings hundreds. Len Hutton replied with an unbeaten 202, but England were made to follow-on and fell, again, to the wiles of Valentine, who took 6-39 to make it an innings victory and a 3-1 series win.

Incredibly, eight of the tour party (Weekes, Worrell, Walcott, Stollmeyer, Rae, Marshall, Gomez and Christiani) all scored more than 1,000 first class runs on the trip, with Everton Weekes totalling an impressive 2310, including seven centuries!

Despite plenty of good support performances, the two stand-out bowlers were the spin twins, Sonny Ramadhin and Alf Valentine. Sonny, the right arm wrist spinner from Trinidad and Tobago, took 135 wickets, whilst the Jamaican slow left-armer bagged 123. Their performances led to celebrations throughout the Caribbean and they were immortalised in the famous song, 'Victory Calypso', by Lord Beginner, which featured the lyrics:

*They gave the crowd plenty fun,*
*Second Test and West Indies won,*
*With those two little pals of mine.*
*Ramadhin and Valentine*

# England v West Indies

(The Trent Bridge Tests)
20, 21, 22, 24, 25 July 1950 (5-day match)
Toss won by England who elected to bat
Umpires: F Chester & H Elliott

## Result: West Indies won by 10 wickets

### England first innings

| RT Simpson | c Walcott b Johnson | 4 |
|---|---|---|
| C Washbrook | c Stollmeyer b Worrell | 3 |
| WGA Parkhouse | c Weekes b Johnson | 13 |
| JG Dewes | c Gomez b Worrell | 0 |
| *NWD Yardley | c Goddard b Valentine | 41 |
| DJ Insole | lbw b Ramadhin | 21 |
| +TG Evans | b Ramadhin | 32 |
| D Shackleton | b Worrell | 42 |
| RO Jenkins | b Johnson | 39 |
| AV Bedser | c Stollmeyer b Valentine | 13 |
| WE Hollies | not out | 2 |
| Extras | (12 lb, 1 nb) | 13 |
| Total | (all out, 98.4 overs) | 223 |

Fall of wickets:
1-6 (Washbrook), 2-18 (Simpson), 3-23 (Parkhouse), 4-25 (Dewes),
5-75 (Insole), 6-105 (Yardley), 7-147 (Evans), 8-174 (Shackleton),
9-191 (Bedser), 10-223 (Jenkins, 98.4 ov)

| West Indies bowling | Ovs | Ms | Runs | Wkts |
|---|---|---|---|---|
| Johnson | 25.4 | 5 | 59 | 3 |
| Worrell | 17 | 4 | 40 | 3 |
| Gomez | 3 | 1 | 9 | 0 |
| Goddard | 6 | 3 | 10 | 0 |
| Ramadhin | 29 | 12 | 49 | 2 |
| Valentine | 18 | 6 | 43 | 2 |

## West Indies first innings

| | | |
|---|---|---:|
| AF Rae | st Evans b Yardley | 68 |
| JB Stollmeyer | c and b Jenkins | 46 |
| RJ Christiani | lbw b Shackleton | 10 |
| FMM Worrell | c Yardley b Bedser | 261 |
| ED Weekes | c and b Hollies | 129 |
| +CL Walcott | b Bedser | 8 |
| GE Gomez | not out | 19 |
| *JDC Goddard | c Yardley b Bedser | 0 |
| HHH Johnson | c Insole b Bedser | 0 |
| S Ramadhin | b Bedser | 2 |
| AL Valentine | b Hollies | 1 |
| Extras | (2 b, 10 lb, 2 nb) | 14 |
| Total | (all out, 174.4 overs) | 558 |

Fall of wickets:
1-77 (Stollmeyer), 2-95 (Christiani), 3-238 (Rae), 4-521 (Worrell), 5-535 (Walcott), 6-537 (Weekes), 7-538 (Goddard), 8-539 (Johnson), 9-551 (Ramadhin), 10-558 (Valentine, 174.4 ov)

### England bowling

| | Ovs | Ms | Runs | Wkts |
|---|---:|---:|---:|---:|
| Bedser | 48 | 9 | 127 | 5 |
| Shackleton | 43 | 7 | 128 | 1 |
| Yardley | 27 | 3 | 82 | 1 |
| Jenkins | 13 | 0 | 73 | 1 |
| Hollies | 43.4 | 8 | 134 | 2 |

## England second innings

| | | |
|---|---|---:|
| RT Simpson | run out | 94 |
| C Washbrook | c Worrell b Valentine | 102 |
| WGA Parkhouse | lbw b Goddard | 69 |
| JG Dewes | lbw b Valentine | 67 |
| *NWD Yardley | b Ramadhin | 7 |
| DJ Insole | st Walcott b Ramadhin | 0 |
| +TG Evans | c Stollmeyer b Ramadhin | 63 |
| D Shackleton | c Weekes b Valentine | 1 |
| RO Jenkins | not out | 6 |
| AV Bedser | b Ramadhin | 2 |
| WE Hollies | lbw b Ramadhin | 0 |
| Extras | (11 b, 10 lb, 2 nb, 2 w) | 25 |
| Total | (all out, 245.2 overs) | 436 |

Fall of wickets:
1-212 (Washbrook), 2-220 (Simpson), 3-326 (Parkhouse), 4-346 (Yardley), 5-350 (Insole), 6-408 (Dewes), 7-410 (Shackleton), 8-434 (Evans), 9-436 (Bedser), 10-436 (Hollies, 245.2 ov)

### West Indies bowling

|           | Ovs  | Ms | Runs | Wkts |
|-----------|------|----|------|------|
| Johnson   | 30   | 5  | 65   | 0    |
| Worrell   | 19   | 8  | 30   | 0    |
| Gomez     | 11   | 3  | 23   | 0    |
| Valentine | 92   | 49 | 140  | 3    |
| Ramadhin  | 81.2 | 25 | 135  | 5    |
| Goddard   | 12   | 6  | 18   | 1    |

## West Indies second innings

| AF Rae        | not out                   | 46  |
|---------------|---------------------------|-----|
| JB Stollmeyer | not out                   | 52  |
| RJ Christiani |                           |     |
| FMM Worrell   |                           |     |
| ED Weekes     |                           |     |
| +CL Walcott   |                           |     |
| GE Gomez      |                           |     |
| *JDC Goddard  |                           |     |
| HHH Johnson   |                           |     |
| S Ramadhin    |                           |     |
| AL Valentine  |                           |     |
| Extras        | (5 nb)                    | 5   |
| Total         | (no wicket, 36.3 overs)   | 103 |

### England bowling

|            | Ovs | Ms | Runs | Wkts |
|------------|-----|----|------|------|
| Bedser     | 11  | 1  | 35   | 0    |
| Shackleton | 6   | 2  | 7    | 0    |
| Hollies    | 7   | 6  | 1    | 0    |
| Jenkins    | 11  | 1  | 46   | 0    |
| Simpson    | 1.3 | 0  | 9    | 0    |

# Sobers arrives

# THE 1957 TOUR

Seven years passed before the West Indies again toured England and the intervening period had brought them mixed success. New Zealand had twice been defeated on overseas tours and India had been tamed in the Caribbean, whilst defeats – home and away – to Australia had gone some way to clarifying the pecking order in world cricket.

The West Indies had missed a good opportunity to defeat England at home in early 1954. They had gone 2-0 up in the five-match series before Len Hutton's side came back to level. Hutton himself had played his part in the final match on that tour, becoming the first England captain to score a double hundred in an overseas Test, whilst Trevor Bailey's 7-34 was equally important in securing the win.

That match, played at Sabina Park, Jamaica, also saw the West Indies give a Test debut to 17-year-old Garfield St Aubrun Sobers of Barbados. With Alf Valentine falling ill just before the match, Sobers was something of a surprise choice to replace him but responded with figures of 4-75 in England's first innings and scored 14 not out and 26 batting at number nine in the order. This was only Sobers' third first class appearance. By the time of the 1957 tour of England, Sobers was an integral part of the side by right, with John Goddard returning as captain after Denis Atkinson had led the side in their previous two series.

Returning to the ranks, Atkinson got his summer off to the best possible start by taking five wickets in each innings as Worcestershire were easily defeated at New Road. The next six matches brought wins over Northamptonshire, Oxford University and Essex, with draws achieved against Cambridge University, MCC and Yorkshire. Only one more fixture remained ahead of the First Test at Edgbaston, a three-day match at Trent Bridge against Nottinghamshire.

The county side gave a debut to another Atkinson – Thomas, a right arm medium fast bowler from Cumberland, who had been playing for the 2nd XI for a couple of seasons. Neither he, nor most of the home attack, which included Aussie leg spinner Bruce Dooland, could do much on the opening day as the West Indians piled on the runs.

Playing in his first ever match at Trent Bridge Sobers, who had opened the batting, made 219 not out as the tour side declared on 489-3, with Clyde Walcott hitting 115, Everton Weekes 68 and Collie Smith a powerful 67 not out. Thanks to half centuries from John Clay, Maurice Hill, Ken Smales and Arthur Jepson, Notts responded with a decent first innings total of their own, 420.

With only time for batting practice on the last day, the West Indies lost Sobers for nought but then witnessed two more top order players get amongst the runs in a stand of 205 for the second wicket. Nyron Asgarali from Trinidad and Tobago, made 130 not out, whilst Guyana's Rohan Kanhai, playing as a wicketkeeper-batsman on his first overseas tour, made 95.

*25, 27, 28 May 1957*
*West Indians 489-3 dec (Sobers 219 no, Walcott 115)*
*and 298-3 (Asgarali 130 no)*
*Notts 420 (Clay 67, Smales 63 no)*
*Match Drawn*

The tourists headed off to Birmingham in good spirits as Edgbaston staged its first Test in 28 years. West Indies gained a first innings lead of 288, thanks to Smith's 161, but then England roared back, with Peter May, 285 not out, and Colin Cowdrey, 154, putting on 411 for the 4th wicket, a record for the home side for any wicket.

Sonny Ramadhin also created history, bowling 98 overs in England's second innings. Late on, England had all of the momentum as the West Indies were reduced to 72-7 before the captain's shook hands on a draw.

The sides then headed to Lord's for a match that was completely dominated by England. Bailey's 7-44 shot out the

West Indies for 127, Cowdrey made 152 out of 424, setting up an innings victory.

So, with England ahead in the series, it was time to come to Nottingham for the Third Test and a match that saw another debutant selected for the home side. Dick Richardson, Worcestershire's left-handed all-rounder, gained selection (for what turned out to be his only Test), playing alongside his brother Peter. This was the first time that England had selected a pair of brothers in the same match since the 1891-92 tour of South Africa, when Alec and George Hearne appeared together – and, bizarrely, a third brother, Frank was in the opposition line-up.

Jim Laker also returned for the Trent Bridge match, instead of Johnny Wardle, but his was just a watching brief for most of the first two days as England piled up a colossal 619-6 declared. Tom Graveney's highest first class score of 258 was the stand-out performance, but he received good support from Peter Richardson (128) and May (104), who played their part in stands of 266 for the second wicket and 207 for the third.

West Indies responded with a huge individual score of their own, as Frank Worrell carried his bat in making 191 not out, following on from the 261 he had scored on his only previous Test appearance on the ground. The follow-on couldn't be saved though and the West Indies were put in again, 247 adrift.

Collie Smith ensured that the match would be drawn with his second century of the series, despite the best efforts of England's new ball bowlers. Brian Statham took 5-118 and Fred Trueman 4-80, to go with his first innings analysis of 5-63.

England went on to win both of the last two Test matches of the summer – and each by an innings – as the powerful line-up of West Indian batting talent failed to find any late-season form. Dismissed for 142 and 132 at Leeds and then 89 and 86 at the Kennington Oval meant a sour end to the 1957 tour and a 3-0 defeat.

# England v West Indies

(The Trent Bridge Tests)
4, 5, 6, 8, 9 July 1957 (5-day match)
Toss won by England who elected to bat
Umpires: JS Buller, FS Lee

## Result: Match Drawn

**England first innings**

| | | |
|---|---|---|
| PE Richardson | c Walcott b Atkinson | 126 |
| DV Smith | c Kanhai b Worrell | 1 |
| TW Graveney | b Smith | 258 |
| *PBH May | lbw b Smith | 104 |
| MC Cowdrey | run out | 55 |
| DW Richardson | b Sobers | 33 |
| +TG Evans | not out | 26 |
| TE Bailey | not out | 3 |
| JC Laker | | |
| FS Trueman | | |
| JB Statham | | |
| Extras | (1 b, 10 lb, 1 nb, 1 w) | 13 |
| Total | (6 wickets, dec., 212 overs) | 619 |

Fall of wickets:
1-14 (Smith), 2-280 (PE Richardson), 3-487 (May), 4-510
(Graveney), 5-573 (DW Richardson), 6-609 (Cowdrey

**West Indies bowling**

| | Ovs | Ms | Runs | Wkts |
|---|---|---|---|---|
| Worrell | 21 | 4 | 79 | 1 |
| Gilchrist | 29 | 3 | 118 | 0 |
| Atkinson | 40 | 7 | 99 | 1 |
| Ramadhin | 38 | 5 | 95 | 0 |
| Valentine | 23 | 4 | 68 | 0 |
| Sobers | 21 | 6 | 60 | 1 |
| Goddard | 15 | 5 | 26 | 0 |
| Smith | 25 | 5 | 61 | 2 |

## West Indies first innings

| | | |
|---|---|---:|
| FMM Worrell | not out | 191 |
| GS Sobers | b Laker | 47 |
| CL Walcott | c and b Laker | 17 |
| +RB Kanhai | c Evans b Bailey | 42 |
| ED Weekes | b Trueman | 33 |
| OG Smith | c Evans b Trueman | 2 |
| DS Atkinson | c Evans b Trueman | 4 |
| *JDC Goddard | c May b Trueman | 0 |
| R Gilchrist | c DW Richardson b Laker | 1 |
| AL Valentine | b Trueman | 1 |
| S Ramadhin | b Statham | 19 |
| Extras | (5 b, 10 lb) | 15 |
| Total | (all out, 160.4 overs) | 372 |

### England bowling

| | Ovs | Ms | Runs | Wkts |
|---|---|---|---|---|
| Statham | 28.4 | 9 | 78 | 1 |
| Trueman | 30 | 8 | 63 | 5 |
| Laker | 62 | 27 | 101 | 3 |
| Bailey | 28 | 9 | 77 | 1 |
| Smith | 12 | 1 | 38 | 0 |

Fall of wickets:
1-87 (Sobers), 2-120 (Walcott), 3-229 (Kanhai), 4-295 (Weekes), 5-297 (Smith), 6-305 (Atkinson), 7-305 (Goddard), 8-314 (Gilchrist), 9-317 (Valentine), 10-372 (Ramadhin, 160.4 ov)

## West Indies second innings (following on)

| | | |
|---|---|---:|
| FMM Worrell | b Statham | 16 |
| GS Sobers | lbw b Trueman | 9 |
| CL Walcott | c Evans b Laker | 7 |
| +RB Kanhai | c Evans b Trueman | 28 |
| ED Weekes | b Statham | 3 |
| OG Smith | b Trueman | 168 |
| DS Atkinson | c Evans b Statham | 46 |
| *JDC Goddard | c Evans b Statham | 61 |
| S Ramadhin | b Trueman | 15 |
| R Gilchrist | b Statham | 0 |
| AL Valentine | not out | 2 |
| Extras | (2 b, 10 lb) | 12 |
| Total | (all out, 148.2 overs) | 367 |

Fall of wickets:
1-22 (Sobers), 2-30 (Worrell), 3-39 (Walcott), 4-56 (Weekes), 5-89 (Kanhai), 6-194 (Atkinson), 7-348 (Goddard), 8-352 (Smith), 9-365 (Ramadhin), 10-367 (Gilchrist, 148.2 ov)

### England bowling

|          | Ovs  | Ms | Runs | Wkts |
|----------|------|----|------|------|
| Statham  | 41.2 | 12 | 118  | 5    |
| Trueman  | 35   | 5  | 80   | 4    |
| Laker    | 43   | 14 | 98   | 1    |
| Smith    | 12   | 5  | 23   | 0    |
| Bailey   | 12   | 3  | 22   | 0    |
| Graveney | 5    | 2  | 14   | 0    |

## England second innings

| PE Richardson | c Kanhai b Gilchrist | 11 |
|---------------|----------------------|----|
| DV Smith | not out | 16 |
| TW Graveney | not out | 28 |
| *PBH May | | |
| MC Cowdrey | | |
| DW Richardson | | |
| +TG Evans | | |
| TE Bailey | | |
| JC Laker | | |
| FS Trueman | | |
| JB Statham | | |
| Extras | (7 b, 2 lb) | 9 |
| Total | (1 wicket, 17 overs) | 64 |

### West Indies bowling

|          | Ovs | Ms | Runs | Wkts |
|----------|-----|----|------|------|
| Worrell  | 7   | 1  | 27   | 0    |
| Gilchrist| 7   | 0  | 21   | 1    |
| Atkinson | 1   | 0  | 1    | 0    |
| Goddard  | 1   | 0  | 2    | 0    |
| Walcott  | 1   | 0  | 4    | 0    |

# CARLTON FORBES

*Date of birth: 9 August 1936 Kingston, Jamaica*
*Died: 28 May 2009 Ocho Rios, Jamaica*

Regulations in force at the time prevented Carlton Forbes from being an even bigger star than he turned out to be. After being recruited in 1959 from club cricket in Middlesbrough, where he was playing in the North Yorks and South Durham League, he was made to wait two years by the TCCB before qualifying to play in the County Championship. Nevertheless, so keen was he to pursue a career in the professional game, he joined Notts and became the leading wicket taker in the 2nd XI.

Given permission by his native Jamaica to sign a full-time contract at Trent Bridge, Carlton was given a first class debut at home to Cambridge University. In a match that has become more memorable for the Australian Keith Miller scoring an unbeaten century on his only appearance for the county, Forbes scored 36 in his only innings – batting at six in the order – and took two wickets in the match, the second of which was Henry Blofeld, later to become an acclaimed cricket broadcaster.

At the time Carlton was seen as a powerful middle order batsman and left arm spinner, but under the tutelage of Bill Voce he gradually lengthened his run, increased his pace and became a more than useful medium fast seamer. In 1960 he played two first class matches, scoring his maiden fifty in another match against the students, at Fenners, as well as appearing against the touring South Africans.

Fully qualified, Carlton proved to be more of a success with the bat in his first season, hitting over 1,000 first class runs. Gradually though his bowling became his strongest suit and he went on to become only the second Notts bowler (after Bruce Dooland) to take more than 100 wickets in three consecutive seasons between 1965 and 1967.

Despite occasional appearances for the International Cavaliers and touring West Indian XIs for testimonial and benefit matches, full international honours evaded Carlton, although he was joined at Trent Bridge by his national skipper, Garfield Sobers, one of the first to benefit from the change in regulation regarding overseas players.

Carlton had received his county cap in 1965 and was given a benefit in 1969, but a year later refused a new contract and went and played for Church in the Lancashire League. By then Carlton had acquired a business – and a nickname. He had opened the New Calypso Club, off Friar Lane in Nottingham, a nightspot that became exceedingly popular with the West Indian community. The owner soon became known to one and all as 'Cha Cha', after the popular dance.

His love of the night-life became part of the Trent Bridge folklore, with stories of him dancing all night and then sleeping it off in the dressing rooms whenever Notts were batting.

Laid-back and immensely likeable to everyone at Trent Bridge, 'Cha Cha' returned to the club during the 1973 season, playing in six more first class matches and a handful of one-dayers before finally calling it a day and returning back to the country of his birth.

Carlton played in 244 first class matches for Notts, scoring 3605 runs at an average of 14.42, with a top score of 86, achieved against Lancashire at Southport in 1961. He bagged 706 wickets at 25.37, with a best of 7-19 at home to Kent in 1966. On 23 occasions he took five wickets in an innings and twice claimed ten in a match.

In 2008 Carlton was diagnosed with cancer and he died at his home in Ocho Rios, Jamaica on 28 May 2009.

# Butchered in '66

# THE 1963 TOUR

Disappointingly, Trent Bridge wasn't awarded any of the 1963 Test matches against the West Indies, with the five games being played at Old Trafford, Lord's, Edgbaston, Headingley and Kennington Oval.

The series opened in Manchester with Lance Gibbs, of Guyana, spinning the West Indies to a 10-wicket victory. Pressure had been put on the home side by a substantial first innings score of 501-6 declared by the tourists, with 182 coming from opening batsman Conrad Hunte, of Barbados, plus 90 from Rohan Kanhai.

Debuting in the match were Surrey's John Edrich for England and two cricketers from Trinidad and Tobago, opening batsman Joey Carew and wicket-keeper Deryck Murray, who would later join Nottinghamshire.

In terms of sheer drama the Second Test at Lord's had it all and went right down to the final ball of the match. At that stage England's last pair were together, with six runs needed for victory. Gloucestershire's David Allen was on strike, having just been joined at the non-striker's end by Colin Cowdrey.

The Kent man had been forced to retire hurt earlier in the innings when struck on the left forearm. X-Rays revealed a break and he was put in plaster. Heroically, he made his way out to the middle, following a run out, intending to bat left handed, but just using his right hand on the bat – if required. As it transpired, Allen blocked the final two balls to secure the draw.

England levelled the series in Birmingham with Trueman's seven-wicket haul in the second innings completely blew the West Indies away, but the tourists hit back to win in Leeds. Sobers scored a ton there, with Nottinghamshire's Brian Bolus scoring 14 and 43 on his Test debut.

2-1 up in the series, the tourists came to Trent Bridge to face Notts ahead of the all-important final Test. With Worrell resting, his vice-captain Conrad Hunte led a side which included Sobers on the ground where he'd scored a double hundred on the previous tour.

The first day went well for the county side, dismissing their visitors for 319, which represented a decent turnaround after Hunte had put on 178 for the first wicket with partner Easton McMorris, Bomber Wells' off-breaks accounting for five of the wickets to fall.

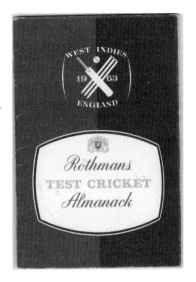

Sobers removed Reg Simpson for nought late on the first evening, allowing Jamaican-born Carlton Forbes to come out as nightwatchman. Forbes fell to the express pace of Wes Hall on the second morning and Notts were soon blown away for 143 and asked to follow on.

Geoff Millman, Notts' wicket-keeper and skipper, had top-scored with 40 in his side's first innings and his 60, together with 75 from Andrew Corran, helped them to 306 second time around.

Chasing just 136, the West Indies ran out of time at 93-3 as they maintained their unbeaten record at Trent Bridge with their seventh draw from ten appearances on the ground.

### 17, 19, 20 August 1963
### West Indians 314 (Hunte 89, McMorris 87, Wells 5-89) and 93-3
### Notts 143 and 306 (Corran 75)
### Match Drawn

The match in Nottingham concluded on Tuesday tea-time, giving the West Indies a limited amount of time before the Final Test of the summer was scheduled to begin at the Kennington Oval on the Thursday morning.

Charlie Griffith, who had been rested for the Trent Bridge match, took 6-71 on the opening day as England fell for 275, which was still good enough for a first innings lead of 29.

Second time around the home team could only make 223, meaning that the series was very much on the line with the West Indians needing to chase down 253. Thanks to Conrad Hunte, with an undefeated 108, supported by 77 from Kanhai, the task became a formality.

The eight-wicket victory not only meant a 3-1 series win for the West Indies, but it also enabled them to become the first holders of The Wisden Trophy – a new piece of silverware awarded to commemorate the hundredth edition of the Wisden Cricketers' Almanack.

Skipper Frank Worrell collected the Trophy and accepted the deserved plaudits for a job well done. Three years earlier he had become the first full-time black captain of the West Indies and had moulded them into the best side on the planet.

The Oval match had been his 51$^{st}$ and final Test but he wouldn't be lost to the game, going on to manage the side as well as being knighted for his services to the game. Wasting little time in announcing his successor, the West Indian selectors appointed Garfield Sobers as the new captain.

# 1966

Since defeating England on their 1963 tour, the West Indies had only played one other series – a home victory over Australia – before returning to defend the Wisden Trophy during the Football World Cup summer of 1966.

Sobers' side contained a fiery pair of new ball strike bowlers, Wes Hall and Charlie Griffith, a world-class spinner in Lance Gibbs, a strong batting line-up, plus the all-round brilliance of the captain himself.

Once more, Trent Bridge was listed to host a Test – the third in the series of five. Additionally, Nottinghamshire would also face the tourists in a match played in early season.

Draws at Worcester, where only 92 overs were possible throughout the three days, and at The Parks, where Rohan Kanhai made 192 not out against Oxford University, had given the touring side a gentle introduction to their programme.

# DERYCK MURRAY

### *Date of birth: 20 May 1943 Port of Spain, Trinidad*

Deryck Murray played in 62 Test matches for the West Indies spread over a 17-year period. His first five Tests, in 1963, preceded a spell in England where he studied at Jesus College, Cambridge and also Nottingham University. His educational commitments enabled him to qualify to play county cricket whilst in England and he joined Notts during 1966, making his debut against Yorkshire at Bramall Lane, Sheffield.

A more than capable right-handed batsman and wicket-keeper, Deryck played a total of 97 firs class matches for Notts, more appearances than he made for any other side during his career. In just his sixth appearance in county cricket he made the highest score of his career, 166 not out, batting at number three in the order against Surrey at the Oval.

In total, Deryck scored 3873 runs for Nottinghamshire, averaging more than 31. Four of his ten career hundreds came as a Notts player and he also claimed 172 dismissals, made up of 157 catches and 15 stumpings.

Returning to his country's international side, he kept wicket during their period of global dominance under Clive Lloyd and was a member of their two World Cup-winning sides in 1975 and 1979.

After retiring from the game, he served as a diplomat in the Foreign Service of Trinidad and Tobago and was a representative to the United Nations in New York. He has also served as President of the Trinidad and Tobago Cricket Board.

The match at Trent Bridge – in theory – should have seen the West Indians approaching their best form ahead of the opening Test match, but again they were thwarted by the rain, which washed out the first day.

Sobers was the star performer on the second day, scoring 153, but too much time had been taken out of the game and the inevitable draw ensued.

*11, 12, 13 May 1966*
*335-7 dec (Sobers 153) and 81-3*
*Notts 259-6 dec (Moore 63)*
*Match Drawn*

It was the end of June before the tourists returned to Trent Bridge to face England in the Third Test match. They arrived holding a 1-0 lead in the series after an innings victory at Old Trafford, where Hunte and Sobers scored hundreds on the way to a total of 484, which was more than enough as Lance Gibbs collected five wickets in each innings to spin the home side to defeat.

MJK Smith, of Warwickshire, had captained England in the opening match of the rubber but was then replaced by Colin Cowdrey for the second Test at Lord's. The home side also brought in Basil D'Oliveira, Worcestershire's South African-born all-rounder, for his debut.

England managed to secure a first innings lead of 86, but it wasn't enough as the tourists then compiled a second innings score of 369-5 declared, with the foundation an unbroken sixth wicket stand of 274 between Sobers (163 not out) and his cousin, Davd Holford, who scored an unbeaten 105 in just his second Test match. Colin Milburn then scored his first international century before the game was closed out as a draw.

Seymour Nurse scored 155 against Essex at Southend in the one fixture squeezed in before the Third Test, where England again introduced a new face, with Kent's left arm spinner Derek Underwood coming in for the first time. No doubt Cowdrey, his county captain, had backed his claim for a place.

The opening day produced 13 wickets, with the West Indies shot out for 235, John Snow and Ken Higgs each taking four wickets. The day ended strongly for the visitors though, as they picked up the wickets of Milburn, Boycott and Russell with only 13 runs on the board.

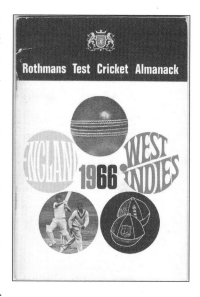

Wickets were harder to come by on the second day, with Tom Graveney assisting his captain towards a fourth wicket partnership of 169. Graveney made 109 before becoming one of Sobers' four victims, whilst Cowdrey fell for 96. A lead of 90 at the halfway stage of the contest at least provided England with the possibility of being able to square the series.

Those aspirations didn't last long as the West Indies made the most of ideal batting conditions on the fourth day. Basil Butcher, a stocky and powerful batsman from Guyana, made the highest score of his career – an unbeaten 209. Sobers' fine form continued with 94 and both Kanhai and Nurse passed fifty, enabling another declaration at 482-5. Underwood's debut went wicketless, although he bowled 45 overs in the match, all but two of them in the second innings.

England began the last day on 30-0, needing a further 363 to win. The target proved immaterial because wickets tumbled at regular intervals all day, with Sobers rotating himself, Hall and Griffiths in supporting Lance Gibbs as the home side were dismissed for 253.

Going 2-0 up in the series, with only two more matches to play meant that the Wisden Trophy would be retained whatever happened in the remaining matches, but winning the series was what concerned Sobers most and he couldn't have demonstrated that better than by his performance at Headingley in the Fourth Test.

Confirming his ranking as the best all-rounder in world cricket, he turned in a stunning display with both bat and ball. His 174, racked up in just four hours, complemented by 137 from Nurse, took the West Indies to 500-9 declared and then Sobers the bowler took 5-41 and 3-39 as England were walloped by an innings. In fairness, Lance Gibbs also played his part, taking 6-39 in England's second innings.

At 3-0 down England would seem to have had little more than pride to play for as the series headed for the Kennington Oval. Looking for the players to show some fight, the selectors ruthlessly rang the changes. Cowdrey was dropped, losing his place as captain to Brian Close, the sparky Yorkshire skipper. Out also went Colin Milburn, Fred Titmus, wicket-keeper Jim Parks and, after just one match, the unfortunate Derek Underwood. Dennis Amiss of Warwickshire was given a debut, with recalls also for John Edrich, Ray Illingworth and John Murray.

Despite a ton from Kanhai, the West Indies were bundled out for a below par 268. England's impressive response totalled 527, with Graveney scoring 165 and wicket-keeper Murray proving to be an inspired selection, making 112 batting at number nine.

Whether the tourists had become a little de-mob happy at having already won the series, or whether they were comprehensively outplayed, is subjective, but any fight they did have disappeared when Sobers was dismissed first ball. He had enjoyed the most magnificent of summers, scoring 722 runs over the five Tests, with three centuries and an average of 103, but he was undone by a bold piece of captaincy from Close.

Positioning himself on the leg side, just a few feet from the bat, Close instructed John Snow to bang one in short at their greatest adversary. Instinctively, Sobers went for the pull, edged the ball into his body and up, obligingly, into the hands of the England captain.

The remainder of the card folded cheaply, leaving England victorious by an innings. The summer had certainly belonged to the nation's footballers but the cricket team – although well beaten – had ended the season with a win.

# England v West Indies

(The Trent Bridge Tests)
30 June, 1, 2, 4, 5 July 1966 (5-day match)
Toss: won by West Indies who elected to bat
Umpires: CS Elliott, A Jepson

## Result: West Indies won by 139 runs

### West Indies first innings

| | | |
|---|---|---|
| CC Hunte | lbw b Higgs | 9 |
| PD Lashley | c Parks b Snow | 49 |
| RB Kanhai | c Underwood b Higgs | 32 |
| BF Butcher | b Snow | 5 |
| SM Nurse | c Illingworth b Snow | 93 |
| *GS Sobers | c Parks b Snow | 3 |
| DAJ Holford | lbw b D'Oliveira | 11 |
| +JL Hendriks | b D'Oliveira | 2 |
| CC Griffith | c Cowdrey b Higgs | 14 |
| WW Hall | b Higgs | 12 |
| LR Gibbs | not out | 0 |
| Extras | (3 b, 2 lb) | 5 |
| Total | (all out, 90.4 overs) | 235 |

Fall of wickets:
1-19 (Hunte), 2-68 (Kanhai), 3-80 (Butcher), 4-140 (Lashley), 5-144 (Sobers), 6-180 (Holford), 7-190 (Hendriks), 8-215 (Nurse), 9-228 (Hall), 10-235 (Griffith, 90.4 ov)

### England bowling

| | Ovs | Ms | Runs | Wkts |
|---|---|---|---|---|
| Snow | 25 | 7 | 82 | 4 |
| Higgs | 25.4 | 3 | 71 | 4 |
| D'Oliveira | 30 | 14 | 51 | 2 |
| Underwood | 2 | 1 | 5 | 0 |
| Illingworth | 8 | 1 | 21 | 0 |

### England first innings

| G Boycott | lbw b Sobers | 0 |
|---|---|---|
| C Milburn | c Sobers b Hall | 7 |
| WE Russell | b Hall | 4 |
| TW Graveney | c Holford b Sobers | 109 |
| *MC Cowdrey | c Hendriks b Griffith | 96 |
| +JM Parks | c Butcher b Sobers | 11 |
| BL D'Oliveira | b Hall | 76 |
| R Illingworth | c Lashley b Griffith | 0 |
| K Higgs | c Lashley b Sobers | 5 |
| JA Snow | b Hall | 0 |
| DL Underwood | not out | 12 |
| Extras | (2 lb, 3 nb) | 5 |
| Total | (all out, 134.3 overs) | 325 |

Fall of wickets:
1-0 (Boycott), 2-10 (Milburn), 3-13 (Russell), 4-182 (Graveney), 5-221 (Parks), 6-238 (Cowdrey), 7-247 (Illingworth), 8-255 (Higgs), 9-260 (Snow), 10-325 (D'Oliveira, 134.3 ov)

### West Indies bowling

| | Ovs | Ms | Runs | Wkts |
|---|---|---|---|---|
| Sobers | 49 | 12 | 90 | 4 |
| Hall | 34.3 | 8 | 105 | 4 |
| Griffith | 20 | 5 | 62 | 2 |
| Gibbs | 23 | 9 | 40 | 0 |
| Holford | 8 | 2 | 23 | 0 |

### West Indies second innings

| CC Hunte | c Graveney b D'Oliveira | 12 |
|---|---|---|
| PD Lashley | lbw b D'Oliveira | 23 |
| RB Kanhai | c Cowdrey b Higgs | 63 |
| BF Butcher | not out | 209 |
| SM Nurse | lbw b Higgs | 53 |
| *GS Sobers | c Underwood b Higgs | 94 |
| DAJ Holford | not out | 17 |
| Extras | (6 lb, 5 w) | 11 |
| Total | (5 wickets, dec, 178 overs) | 482 |

+JL Hendriks, CC Griffith, WW Hall, LR Gibbs did not bat

Fall of wickets:
1-29 (Hunte), 2-65 (Lashley), 3-175 (Kanhai), 4-282 (Nurse), 5-455 (Sobers)

## England bowling

|            | Ovs | Ms | Runs | Wkts |
|------------|-----|----|------|------|
| Snow       | 38  | 10 | 117  | 0    |
| Higgs      | 38  | 6  | 109  | 3    |
| D'Oliveira | 34  | 8  | 77   | 2    |
| Underwood  | 43  | 15 | 86   | 0    |
| Illingworth| 25  | 7  | 82   | 0    |

## England second innings

| G Boycott      | c Sobers b Griffith    | 71  |
|----------------|------------------------|-----|
| C Milburn      | c Griffith b Hall      | 12  |
| WE Russell     | c Sobers b Gibbs       | 11  |
| TW Graveney    | c Hendriks b Griffith  | 32  |
| *MC Cowdrey    | c Sobers b Gibbs       | 32  |
| +JM Parks      | c Lashley b Hall       | 7   |
| BL D'Oliveira  | lbw b Griffith         | 54  |
| R Illingworth  | c Lashley b Sobers     | 4   |
| K Higgs        | c Sobers b Gibbs       | 4   |
| JA Snow        | b Griffith             | 3   |
| DL Underwood   | not out                | 10  |
| Extras         | (8 b, 2 lb, 3 nb)      | 13  |
| Total          | (all out, 108.3 overs) | 253 |

Fall of wickets:
1-32 (Milburn), 2-71 (Russell), 3-125 (Boycott), 4-132 (Graveney), 5-142 (Parks), 6-176 (Cowdrey), 7-181 (Illingworth), 8-222 (Higgs), 9-240 (D'Oliveira), 10-253 (Snow, 108.3 ov)

## West Indies bowling

|          | Ovs  | Ms | Runs | Wkts |
|----------|------|----|------|------|
| Sobers   | 31   | 6  | 71   | 1    |
| Hall     | 16   | 3  | 52   | 2    |
| Griffith | 13.3 | 3  | 34   | 4    |
| Gibbs    | 48   | 16 | 83   | 3    |

# SIR GARFIELD SOBERS

*Date of birth: 28 July 1936 Bridgetown, Barbados*

Certainly the greatest player of his generation, and undoubtedly one of the leading all-rounders ever to have graced the game, Sir Garfield Sobers played for Nottinghamshire between 1968 and 1974. Captain of the West Indies, Garry's acquisition was seen as a pioneering move by the club's committee, who were desperate to end a lengthy period of on-field disappointment.

He was 31-years-old when he joined Notts and had played Lancashire League and Staffordshire League cricket during previous English summers before a change in the qualifying regulations allowed overseas players to move into the county game.

Holder (at the time) of the highest score in Test Match cricket – his 365 not out coming against Pakistan in Kingston, Jamaica in 1958 – he was handed the captaincy of his new county ahead of his debut, at home to Middlesex in May 1968. After an opening day wash-out, his first day of action as a Notts player couldn't have gone much better, with figures of 5-25 followed by a score of 59 not out.

Garry had enjoyed his previous visits to Nottingham as a West Indies player, scoring 219 and 153 in separate matches against the county, as well as hitting 94 in the 1966 Test against England there, but whilst his arrival didn't necessarily bring an immediate change in the fortunes of the side, he nevertheless turned in some outstanding performances himself.

He played a total of 107 first class matches for Notts, scoring over 7,000 runs, with 18 centuries at an average of 48.9. Capable of bowling in a variety of differing styles, from genuinely quick to slightly slower seam and swing, to much slower orthodox left arm spin, and also switching to chinamen and googlies, his haul of 281 wickets came at an average of 25 and included a best of 7-69.

Of course no mention of Sobers' time with Notts would be complete without a recap of his most celebrated act. Skippering his side away against Glamorgan at the St Helen's Ground in Swansea, he achieved cricketing immortality by hitting six sixes in one over, becoming the first player to ever do so.

Sobers retired at the end of the 1974 season and in the following New Year's Honours List he was awarded a knighthood for his services to cricket.

# Smedley's Double

# 1969-1973

Having had such a successful tour three seasons earlier, the West Indies arrived in England during a period of transition. They had lost the Wisden Trophy during a turbulent home series, in early 1968, when the one positive result came after what was seen as a fairly generous declaration by Sobers in the fourth Test at Port of Spain. A 3-1 loss to Australia a year later and a drawn trip to New Zealand had hardly been ideal preparation for their return to these shores, sharing a split summer with the Kiwis.

England won the First Test convincingly at Old Trafford, where Maurice Foster, Vanburn Holder and Jon Shepherd all made their international bows for the visitors. Straight after that crushing defeat came a tour match at Nottingham, their only scheduled match at Trent Bridge. With Sobers rested against his home county, his deputy Basil Butcher led the side on the ground where he'd hit a double century three years earlier.

On winning the toss, he saw Charlie Davis, Clive Lloyd, Roy Fredericks and Steve Camacho all make half centuries out of a declared total of 323-5, with left arm quick Barry Stead shining for the county side, collecting 4-67 from 23 overs. Another left-armer, Carlton Forbes, grabbed the other wicket against his countrymen.

Mike Smedley scored an unbeaten 103 in Nottinghamshire's reply before Brian Bolus declared, 53 behind, early on the final morning. West Indies failed to make the most of the opportunity for some batting practice, losing half their side for 122, with Graham Frost taking his first three wickets for Notts.

*18, 19, 20 June 1969*
*West Indians 323-5 dec (Davis 82, Lloyd 79) and 122-5*
*Notts 270-5 dec (Smedley 103 not out)*

Things didn't really improve for Sobers' side during the remainder of their stay, although the Lord's Test was nicely poised and could have gone either way had another hour of play been possible.

Chasing 332, the home team were 295-7 at stumps. Earlier in the contest Yorkshire's John Hampshire had become the first Englishman to score a century, whilst making a Test match debut at Lord's.

The Third Test was again fairly tight, with England winning by only 30 runs as the West Indies fell for 272 in their second innings, chasing 303.

A home series against India failed to revive Caribbean confidence, with Sunil Gavaskar making a spectacular entrance into top-flight cricket. Only given his debut in the second match of the series, he scored 774 runs, at an average of 154.8 and with four centuries, including a top score of 220 not out.

Five drawn Tests against New Zealand in 1972 took Sobers run of consecutive appearances to 85 for the West Indies, but knee surgery then ruled him out of the visit by Australia twelve months later. Rohan Kanhai took over as captain but, despite the series being closely-fought, wins in Trinidad and Guyana brought Australia a 2-0 triumph. Sobers was declared fit enough to make the 1973 three Test tour of England, but Kanhai retained the captaincy.

Rain ruined the tour opener against Essex and then the captain and Roy Fredericks scored hundreds against Hampshire, who included a couple of West Indians of their own, batsman Gordon Greenidge and the tearaway fast bowler from Antigua, Andy Roberts.

The first set-back came in a match against a strong DH Robins' XI at Eastbourne, with Geoff Boycott having a fine match, scoring 114 and then 74 not out, as he and Dennis Amiss, 95 not out, chased down 172 for a ten-wicket win.

With the First Test still three weeks away, the West Indies next faced Nottinghamshire at Trent Bridge. The county side gave a first class debut to young all-rounder Trevor Tunnicliffe, whilst they also introduced Dilip Doshi, an experienced Indian slow left-armer spinner, for the first time. Doshi would later go on to make 33 Test appearances.

Lance Gibbs captained the West Indies, whilst his opposite number, Mike Smedley, was one of three batsmen blown away by Bernard Julien's new ball burst. The left-armer also sent back Paul Todd and Derek Randall. Opener Mike Harris withstood the early onslaught and went on reach 106, but he had little support as the innings folded for just 223. Former Notts gloveman Deryck Murray was back in the international fold and took four catches and a stumping on his old ground.

Carlton Forbes dismissed Roy Fredericks late on the first day, but resuming on Monday morning after the Sunday rest day, Guyana's Alvin Kallicharran played a majestic innings of 124, supported by an unbeaten 81 from Maurice Foster, which helped build a substantial first innings lead.

Keith Boyce removed both Harris and Randall for nought when Notts batted again – Randall making a pair in the match – but Smedley, as he had done four years earlier, went on to complete a three figure score against the touring side. Bob White's 80 saw Notts up to 292 but a target of 165 was never likely to be enough and 80s from Fredericks and Rowe wrapped up a nine wicket win.

*30 June, 2, 3 July 1973*
*Notts 223 (Harris 106) and 292 (Smedley 110)*
*West Indians 351-6 dec (Kallicharran 124)*
*and 166-1 (Rowe 84, Fredericks 82 no)*
*West Indians won by 9 wickets*

After going 20 Tests without a single victory, the West Indies won by 158 runs at the Kennington Oval to trigger a 2-0 series success. Keith Boyce's 11 wickets in the match, plus a ton from Clive Lloyd, were instrumental, although a ton on debut from Lancashire's Frank Hayes was one consolation for England.

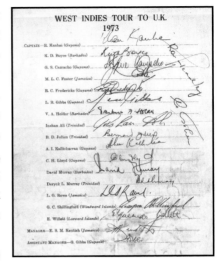

The Second Test was drawn, Fredericks making 150 in the first innings and Lloyd 94 in the second for the West Indies, with Geoff Boycott unwittingly becoming embroiled in a moment of controversy.

He had been forced to retire hurt on two occasions and came out again as the last batsman and ended on 56 not out. However, during the earlier part of his innings the West Indies had appealed for a catch behind by Murray. The following morning, the third of the match, umpire Arthur Fagg refused to stand for the first over of the day in protest at Kanhai's dissent regarding the not out decision. Former player and umpire Alan Oakman deputised briefly.

There was neither controversy, nor doubt, at Lord's where the West Indies clinched the rubber with victory by an innings and 226 runs, their largest success over England to that point.

In a first innings score of 652-8 declared Rohan Kanhai, with 157, and Garfield Sobers, with 150 not out, scored their final Test match hundreds, and then Bernard Julien, 121, his first. England were dismissed for 233 and 193 as the Wisden Trophy again changed hands.

# NIRMAL NANAN

*Date of birth: 19 August 1951 Preysal, Trinidad*

Nirmal Nanan was a right-handed batsman and a leg break and googly bowler who featured for Nottinghamshire during the early 1970s.

Hailing from Trinidad and Tobago, he had played representative cricket as a youngster and made one first class appearance in his homeland. Appearing for South Trinidad against North Trinidad in 1970 he scored 12 and 16 with the bat and grabbed a couple of wickets, the first of which was Joey Carew, a West Indian Test batsman.

Moving to England, he played a season of second eleven cricket for Notts in 1971, although he did make his first team debut against Oxford University in The Parks.

In his second innings he scored 72 and then went on to take 3-12 from just three overs. Both performances would ultimately prove to be his best figures for the county.

Nirmal's championship debut came in 1972, but he was unable to either cement a regular place in the side or nail down a specific role, being shuffled up and down the order at will.

Over the next decade he made a total of just 32 first class appearances for Notts, scoring 846 runs at an average of slightly under sixteen, but he was seldom called upon to bowl. In One Day cricket he also played in 32 matches for Nottinghamshire and, perhaps fittingly, saved his finest performance for his final match.

Playing in a Benson and Hedges Group match against Derbyshire at Trent Bridge, he opened the batting and was eventually run out for 93 in a huge Notts win, earning him the Man of the Match award.

Nirmal returned to Trinidad and made one further first class appearance, playing for South and Central Trinidad, a side captained by his nephew Rangy Nanan, who had played one Test for the West Indies in Pakistan in 1980.

# HARRY LATCHMAN

## *Date of birth: 26 July 1943 Kingston, Jamaica*

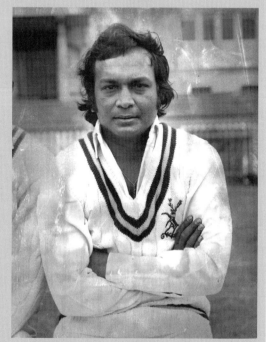

Harry Latchman was born in Jamaica but moved to England with his family as a young child and went to school in White City, West London. A right handed batsman and leg spin bowler, he was invited to join Middlesex and played for their second team from 1963, making his first team debut two seasons later.

His best season was 1968, when he took 88 wickets at an average of 18.88, and he went on to take exactly 400 wickets for Middlesex from 170 outings, with a top score of 96 with the bat.

In 1974 he brought his cheery smile and engaging personality to Trent Bridge, where he spent three seasons in the first team. He played in 40 first class matches for his second county, scoring 651 runs and taking 81 wickets.

Harry's top score of 78 came in a winning cause at Fenner's, against Cambridge University, whilst his best performance with the ball was 7-65, secured against Essex at Ilford.

After leaving Notts, Harry then played for Cambridgeshire in the Minor Counties championship before pursuing a career in the coaching side of the game.

# Viv's double makes Greig eat his words

# 1976

Clive Hubert Lloyd of Guyana had been a regular in the West Indies side since 1966 and was seen as the most logical replacement to succeed Rohan Kanhai as West Indies' skipper. Both Kanhai and Garfield Sobers had bowed out of Test cricket after a home draw against England, noticeable for Andy Roberts' emergence into the side and Lawrence Rowe's brilliant 302 at Kingston.

Lloyd's reign began with a series victory in India. Gordon Greenidge registered a century on his debut in the opening Test and Vivian Richards weighed in with a mightily impressive 192 not out in the next match after missing out in the first.

From a position of dominance at 2-0, the visitors were pegged back level with losses in the third and fourth matches, setting the series up for a thrilling finale in the last Test in Bombay. Lloyd made 242 not out, Roy Fredericks added 104, Alvin Kallicharran 98 and Deryck Murray 91 as the West Indies topped 600 on their way to clinching the series.

1975 saw the inaugural World Cup competition, won by the West Indies, who defeated Australia in the Final, but the Aussies gained revenge in the longer format by taming Lloyd's Test side 5-1 in 1975-76. Michael Holding, a young quick bowler from Jamaica, had broken into the side and the development of his new ball partnership with Andy Roberts was keenly anticipated.

The warm-up matches on the 1976 tour did exactly what they were designed to do, bringing runs for all of the top order batsmen – Richards scored tons against Hampshire and the MCC, with Lloyd, Gomes, King and Greenidge also scoring hundreds – whilst there were five wicket hauls for Julien and Holder, twice each, as well as the spinner Padmore and the fast bowler Daniel. Additionally, the side had accrued confidence from four wins and two draws from the six matches played.

The final pre-Test game had been at Hove against a Sussex side that featured Tony Greig, the new England captain. He had made just four in his one visit to the middle in the tour match, becoming one of Bernard Julien's seven victims. As that match drew to its conclusion Greig conducted an interview, with the BBC *Sportsnight* programme, looking ahead to the forthcoming series.

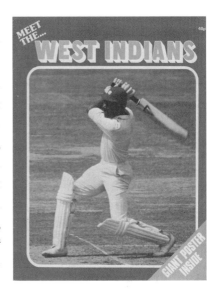

During the previous winter, during a spell playing grade cricket for Waverley, in the Bondi Beach area of Sydney, the England captain had kept a firm eye on the Australia v West Indies series. Clearly he had formulated a few battle plans of his own, but he would have been better advised to keep them to himself.

Instead, on interview, Greig made the point that if you let the West Indians get on top then they are magnificent cricketers. He went on to add: "But if they're down, they grovel, and I intend, with the help of Closey and a few others, to make them grovel."

The use of the word 'grovel' was instantly seized upon by the media and by the West Indian team. For the English captain, Greig – a South African by birth – to use the word 'grovel', with all its racial connotations, meant that the series would begin with an atmosphere akin to a tinderbox – likely to combust with only the slightest provocation. Viv Richards wrote, in his excellent autobiography, *Sir Vivian* (Michael Joseph), that this was the greatest motivational speech Greig could have done for firing the West Indian side up.

Greig's reference to 'Closey' was confirmation that Brian Close would definitely be recalled to the England team for the Trent Bridge Test. Now 35, he hadn't played Test cricket for nine years, since captaining England to victory over Pakistan at the Kennington Oval in August 1967. A typically gritty 88 in a tour match a fortnight earlier had shown the selectors that Close was in decent nick and was up for the fight against the West Indies.

His return meant that he would slot into a fairly senior top four, alongside 38-year-old John Edrich, 34-year-old David Steele and Middlesex's captain Mike Brearley, also 34, who was brought in for his Test debut. Additionally, England had three more players over 30 years of age in their side in John Snow, Alan Knott and Derek Underwood. West Indies selected Wayne Daniel ahead of Holding, whilst Larry Gomes was given a Test debut in place of Lawrence Rowe.

Lloyd won the toss and had no hesitation in batting first. Greenidge made 22 and Fredericks 42, but their dismissals left Vivian Richards and Alvin Kallicharran together soon after lunch.

Both had enjoyed themselves on previous visits to Nottingham – Kallicharran had scored 124 on the previous tour in 1973, whilst a year later Richards had scored a brilliant century for Somerset to win a John Player League match against Nottinghamshire.

So, comfortable in their surroundings, and with a noisy West Indian following in the crowd, they combined beautifully to leave England wicketless for the second half of the day. Richards' century came from 144 deliveries and at stumps he was on 143, with Kalli – as the scoreboard called him – on a workmanlike 52.

The onslaught really gained momentum on the second day as Richards sped to his first Test double hundred and beyond. With 232 to his name he hoisted Underwood to long on, where Greig took a well-judged catch to signify the start of a lengthy and well-deserved standing ovation.

Kalliacharran fell to the same bowler shortly afterwards, just three runs short of a century of his own. The third-wicket stand between the pair had materialised 303 runs. Bearing that in mind, England did reasonably well to take the last eight wickets for just 86 as the West Indies closed on 494.

One over was safely negotiated at the end of the second day, but the third morning brought an immediate breakthrough, with Brearley falling for nought on debut, edging his fourth delivery, from Julien, to Richards at slip. Close also failed, but Edrich batted for three hours in making 37 and then Steele and Woolmer put on 121 together for the fourth wicket as they took England to 221-3 at the close of the third day.

Refreshed after the rest day, the West Indies' attack immediately gained the upper hand on the Monday morning. Steele hooked a short delivery from Daniel straight into the hands of long leg, and then came a moment that the noisy Caribbean supporters celebrated with relish. Greig, under intense pressure and scrutiny after his pre-match comments, was beaten for pace and clean bowled without scoring by a hostile delivery from Roberts. Woolmer's 82 ensured that the follow-on had been saved but the West Indies began their second innings 162 ahead.

Greenidge had an injured leg and was allowed to bat with a runner, although umpires Dickie Bird and Tom Spencer intervened when Collis King came out to do the job. King wasn't even playing in the match! Larry Gomes took over instead. Pushing for quick runs, the West Indies reached 176-5, with Richards again dominant in making 63, before Lloyd declared.

Set 339 to win in five and a quarter hours, England were content to bat sensibly and safely to ensure the series would remain level going into the next match.

# England v West Indies

(The Trent Bridge Tests)
3, 4, 5, 7, 8 June 1976 (5-day match)
Toss: won by West Indies, who elected to bat
Umpires: HD Bird, TW Spencer

## Result: Match drawn

## West Indies first innings

| | | |
|---|---|---|
| RC Fredericks | c Hendrick b Greig | 42 |
| CG Greenidge | c Edrich b Hendrick | 22 |
| IVA Richards | c Greig b Underwood | 232 |
| AI Kallicharran | c Steele b Underwood | 97 |
| *CH Lloyd | c Hendrick b Underwood | 16 |
| BD Julien | c Knott b Old | 21 |
| HA Gomes | c Close b Underwood | 0 |
| +DL Murray | c Close b Snow | 19 |
| VA Holder | not out | 19 |
| AME Roberts | b Old | 1 |
| WW Daniel | c Knott b Old | 4 |
| Extras | (12 lb, 8 nb, 1 w) | 21 |
| Total | (all out, 153.3 overs) | 494 |

Fall of wickets:

1-36 (Greenidge), 2-105 (Fredericks), 3-408 (Richards), 4-423 (Kallicharran), 5-432 (Lloyd), 6-432 (Gomes), 7-458 (Julien), 8-481 (Murray), 9-488 (Roberts), 10-494 (Daniel, 153.3 ov)

### England bowling

| | Ovs | Ms | Runs | Wkts |
|---|---|---|---|---|
| Snow | 31 | 5 | 123 | 1 |
| Hendrick | 24 | 7 | 59 | 1 |
| Old | 34.3 | 7 | 80 | 3 |

| | | | | |
|---|---|---|---|---|
| Greig | 27 | 4 | 82 | 1 |
| Woolmer | 10 | 2 | 47 | 0 |
| Underwood | 27 | 8 | 82 | 4 |

## England first innings

| | | |
|---|---|---|
| JH Edrich | c Murray b Daniel | 37 |
| JM Brearley | c Richards b Julien | 0 |
| DS Steele | c Roberts b Daniel | 106 |
| DB Close | c Murray b Daniel | 2 |
| RA Woolmer | lbw b Julien | 82 |
| *AW Greig | b Roberts | 0 |
| +APE Knott | c sub (CL King) b Holder | 9 |
| CM Old | b Daniel | 33 |
| JA Snow | not out | 20 |
| DL Underwood | c Murray b Holder | 0 |
| M Hendrick | c Daniel b Fredericks | 5 |
| Extras | (5 b, 1 lb, 29 nb, 3 w) | 38 |
| Total | (all out, 134.4 overs) | 332 |

Fall of wickets:
1-0 (Brearley), 2-98 (Edrich), 3-105 (Close), 4-226 (Steele), 5-229 (Greig), 6-255 (Knott), 7-278 (Woolmer), 8-279 (Underwood), 9-318 (Old), 10-332 (Hendrick, 134.4 ov)

### West Indies bowling

| | Ovs | Ms | Runs | Wkts |
|---|---|---|---|---|
| Roberts | 34 | 15 | 53 | 1 |
| Julien | 34 | 9 | 75 | 2 |
| Holder | 25 | 5 | 66 | 2 |
| Daniel | 23 | 8 | 53 | 4 |
| Fredericks | 8.4 | 2 | 24 | 1 |
| Richards | 3 | 1 | 8 | 0 |
| Gomes | 4 | 1 | 8 | 0 |
| Lloyd | 3 | 1 | 7 | 0 |

## West Indies second innings

| | | |
|---|---|---|
| RC Fredericks | b Snow | 15 |
| CG Greenidge | c and b Old | 23 |
| IVA Richards | lbw b Snow | 63 |
| *CH Lloyd | c Brearley b Snow | 21 |
| BD Julien | c Hendrick b Snow | 13 |
| AI Kallicharran | not out | 29 |
| HA Gomes | | |
| +DL Murray | | |
| VA Holder | | |
| AME Roberts | | |
| WW Daniel | | |
| Extras | (6 lb, 4 nb, 2 w) | 12 |
| Total | (5 wkts, dec., 36 ovs) | 176 |

Fall of wickets:
1-33 (Fredericks), 2-77 (Greenidge), 3-109 (Lloyd), 4-124 (Julien),
5-176 (Richards, 36 ov)

### England bowling

| | Ovs | Ms | Runs | Wkts |
|---|---|---|---|---|
| Hendrick | 7 | 2 | 22 | 0 |
| Snow | 11 | 2 | 53 | 4 |
| Underwood | 7 | 3 | 9 | 0 |
| Old | 10 | 0 | 64 | 1 |
| Greig | 1 | 0 | 16 | 0 |

## England second innings

| | | |
|---|---|---|
| JH Edrich | not out | 76 |
| JM Brearley | c Murray b Holder | 17 |
| DS Steele | c Julien b Roberts | 6 |
| DB Close | not out | 36 |
| RA Woolmer | | |
| *AW Greig | | |
| +APE Knott | | |
| CM Old | | |

JA Snow
DL Underwood
M Hendrick
Extras                   (9 b, 10 nb, 2 w)                    21
Total                    (2 wickets, 78 overs)              156

Fall of wickets:
1-38 (Brearley), 2-55 (Steele)

### West Indies bowling

|              | Ovs | Ms | Runs | Wkts |
|--------------|-----|----|------|------|
| Roberts      | 9   | 3  | 20   | 1    |
| Julien       | 16  | 8  | 19   | 0    |
| Daniel       | 10  | 2  | 20   | 0    |
| Holder       | 12  | 6  | 12   | 1    |
| Fredericks   | 9   | 1  | 21   | 0    |
| Richards     | 3   | 1  | 7    | 0    |
| Gomes        | 9   | 1  | 18   | 0    |
| Kallicharran | 10  | 3  | 18   | 0    |

The English summer of 1976 was one of the warmest on record, and as the temperature rose, so did the quality of the West Indies cricket.

Lord's produced another drawn contest, with Roy Fredericks scoring the only century of the match and Andy Roberts claiming five-wicket hauls in each England innings. Derek Underwood's 5-39 helped his side into a first innings lead of 68, but the match eventually petered out on the fifth evening, with West Indies closing on 241-6, chasing 332.

Old Trafford produced the first of three straight West Indian successes, with Gordon Greenidge hitting a hundred in each innings of the match and Richards getting his second century of the series. Michael Holding, who had replaced Daniel for the second Test and kept his place, blew England away for 71 in the first innings by taking five of the wickets to fall and Roberts' 6-37 accounted for the home side in their second knock.

At Leeds Greenidge and Fredericks each reached three figures, putting on 192 for the first wicket on the opening day. England found two centurions of their own in Greig and Knott, but the West Indies' victory ensured that the Wisden Trophy would be retained.

Richards' 291 at the Kennington Oval has frequently been described as one of the greatest Test innings of all-time and took his aggregate for the series to 829 runs. Warwickshire's Dennis Amiss made 203 in England's first innings, but he fell to Michael Holding in each innings, who, with figures of 8-92 and 6-57, became the first West Indian to take more than twelve wickets in a Test.

West Indies then won all three One Day Internationals, leaving them with just two end of tour fixtures to play, the first of them at Trent Bridge against Nottinghamshire.

Nirmal Nanan, born in Trinidad, played for Notts, whilst Deryck Murray again played for the tourists against his former county, but neither featured strongly in a match that seemed about to produce a surprise result. For the first time in 70 years it appeared as if the tourists were destined to taste defeat in Nottingham. The home side made 244 first time around, thanks primarily to 85 from Derek Randall and 59 from opener Paul Todd.

Notts gave a debut to triallist Kenny Watson, a South African-born seamer, and he impressed in picking up four cheap wickets as the West Indies were skittled out for just 81 in reply. The performance was made the more impressive by the fact that medium pace bowler Phil Wilkinson left the field after just two overs.

With only a now-depleted attack at his disposal, home captain Mike Smedley elected not to enforce the follow-on, but his own side capitulated badly against the slow left arm spin of Raphick Jumadeen, who took ten wickets in the match.

Nevertheless, a victory target of 310 seemed a testing one at the outset. That theory was quickly disproved as Greenidge launched a violent counter-attack, scoring the quickest century of the season – coming up in 69 minutes with 13 fours and four sixes. King was almost as brutal and the target was reached in 43.5 overs.

*1, 2, 3 September 1976*
*Notts 244 (Randall 85, Jumadeen 4-30)*
*and 146 (Jumadeen 6-40)*
*West Indians 81 (Watson 4-23) and 313-5*
*(Greenidge 122, King 111)*
*West Indians won by 5 wickets*

# The 1979 World Cup

Having won the inaugural competition four years earlier, the West Indies retained their World Cup crown by defeating England in the 1979 final at Lord's. En-route, they played their first One Day International at Trent Bridge.

Barring a huge mathematical improbability both they, and opponents New Zealand, were already assured of their semi-final berths. Kiwi skipper Mark Burgess won the toss and elected to field and would have been content as his side restricted the holders to 244-7 from their 60 over allocation.

Nottinghamshire supporters had some home interest in the contest, with Richard Hadlee spearheading the New Zealand challenge, but an unbeaten 73 from captain Clive Lloyd, sufficient to secure him the Man of the Match award, plus 65 at the top of the order from Greenidge, saw the West Indies to their victory target. Hadlee, batting at eight on the card, top scored with 42 in the chase, but the all-pace attack of Holding, Roberts, Garner, Croft and King limited the underdogs to 212-9.

A 43-run victory over Pakistan in the semi final took the West Indies to Lord's, where they then had the better of England, who had defeated New Zealand in their own last four match.

*16 June 1979*
*Trent Bridge*
*West Indies 244-7 (Lloyd 73 not out)*
*New Zealand 212-9*
*West Indies won by 32 runs*

# Narrow victory sets up series win

# 1980

The 1970s had ended with the world game being split due to the emergence of Kerry Packer's World Series Cricket and the respective boards suspending players who had been involved.

By the time of the West Indies 1980 tour to England most of those issues had been resolved and the tourists were now acclaimed as the most formidable side on the planet and were close to full strength for a five Test series, the first of which would be held at Trent Bridge.

Having been in the UK for over a month, the tourists were nicely warmed up after a succession of county fixtures, both three-day and one-day, and they had also drawn a two match One Day International series against England.

Desmond Haynes had replaced Roy Fredericks as Greenidge's opening partner and Malcolm Marshall had become the latest to emerge from the conveyor belt of express bowlers, joining Roberts, Holding and Garner as the most potent battery of quickies ever assembled.

England began the summer programme by putting a new man in charge, Somerset's talismanic all-rounder Ian Botham. Bob Woolmer and Alan Knott had been welcomed back into the fold after their defection to World Series Cricket over the previous three years and there was also a debutant batsman in the top order, Kent's Chris Tavare.

Botham won his first toss and opted to bat, but prodigious movement off the seam troubled his men all day on their way to being dismissed for a disappointing 263, with only the captain passing fifty and Roberts taking 5-72. Richards, Greenidge and Deryck Murray all made half centuries when the West Indies batted, edging them to a score of 308 and a first innings lead of 45.

Only Geoff Boycott, with 75, could get to grips with the conditions or the bowling as England again fell cheaply, leaving the West Indies to score 208. A 65-minute cameo from Viv Richards, during which he struck eight majestic fours on his way to 48, looked to make the result a formality, but his departure meant that 99 were required on the final day, with eight wickets left.

Mike Hendrick – later to join Nottinghamshire – dismissed Faoud Bacchus at the start of play on the fifth morning and the nerves began to intensify in the visitor's dressing room as wickets tumbled steadily.

Bob Willis bowled beautifully, with great energy and control, as only Haynes remained of the recognised batsmen. He inched his side to within three of victory but was then eighth man out for 62. Run out by a direct hit from Peter Willey, he left the field in tears but could celebrate moments later as Roberts hit the winning runs in one of the tightest Test finishes for some time.

# England v West Indies

(The Trent Bridge Tests)
5, 6, 7, 9, 10 June 1980 (5-day match)
Toss: won by England, who elected to bat
Umpires: DJ Constant, DO Oslear

## Result: West Indies won by 2 wickets

### England first innings

| | | |
|---|---|---|
| GA Gooch | c Murray b Roberts | 17 |
| G Boycott | c Murray b Garner | 36 |
| CJ Tavaré | b Garner | 13 |
| RA Woolmer | c Murray b Roberts | 46 |
| DI Gower | c Greenidge b Roberts | 20 |
| *IT Botham | c Richards b Garner | 57 |
| P Willey | b Marshall | 13 |

| +APE Knott | lbw b Roberts | 6 |
| JK Lever | c Richards b Holding | 15 |
| RGD Willis | b Roberts | 8 |
| M Hendrick | not out | 7 |
| Extras | (7 b, 11 lb, 4 nb, 3 w) | 25 |
| Total | (all out, 91.5 overs) | 263 |

Fall of wickets:

1-27 (Gooch), 2-72 (Tavaré), 3-74 (Boycott), 4-114 (Gower), 5-204 (Botham), 6-208 (Woolmer), 7-228 (Willey), 8-246 (Knott), 9-254 (Willis), 10-263 (Lever, 91.5 ov)

### West Indies bowling

| | Ovs | Ms | Runs | Wkts |
|---|---|---|---|---|
| Roberts | 25 | 7 | 72 | 5 |
| Holding | 23.5 | 7 | 61 | 1 |
| Marshall | 19 | 3 | 52 | 1 |
| Richards | 1 | 0 | 9 | 0 |
| Garner | 23 | 9 | 44 | 3 |

### West Indies first innings

| CG Greenidge | c Knott b Hendrick | 53 |
| DL Haynes | c Gower b Willis | 12 |
| IVA Richards | c Knott b Willis | 64 |
| SFAF Bacchus | c Botham b Willis | 30 |
| AI Kallicharran | b Botham | 17 |
| +DL Murray | b Willis | 64 |
| *CH Lloyd | c Knott b Lever | 9 |
| MD Marshall | c Tavaré b Gooch | 20 |
| AME Roberts | lbw b Botham | 21 |
| J Garner | c Lever b Botham | 2 |
| MA Holding | not out | 0 |
| Extras | (1 b, 9 lb, 4 nb, 2 w) | 16 |
| Total | (all out, 91.1 overs) | 308 |

Fall of wickets:
1-19 (Haynes), 2-107 (Greenidge), 3-151 (Bacchus), 4-165
(Richards), 5-208 (Kallicharran), 6-227 (Lloyd), 7-265 (Marshall),
8-306 (Roberts), 9-308 (Garner), 10-308 (Murray, 91.1 ov)

**England bowling**

|          | Ovs  | Ms | Runs | Wkts |
|----------|------|----|------|------|
| Willis   | 20.1 | 5  | 82   | 4    |
| Lever    | 20   | 2  | 76   | 1    |
| Hendrick | 19   | 4  | 69   | 1    |
| Willey   | 5    | 3  | 4    | 0    |
| Botham   | 20   | 6  | 50   | 3    |
| Gooch    | 7    | 2  | 11   | 1    |

**England second innings**

| GA Gooch    | run out                    | 27  |
|-------------|----------------------------|-----|
| G Boycott   | b Roberts                  | 75  |
| CJ Tavaré   | c Richards b Garner        | 4   |
| RA Woolmer  | c Murray b Roberts         | 29  |
| DI Gower    | lbw b Garner               | 1   |
| *IT Botham  | c Richards b Roberts       | 4   |
| P Willey    | b Marshall                 | 38  |
| +APE Knott  | lbw b Marshall             | 7   |
| JK Lever    | c Murray b Garner          | 4   |
| RGD Willis  | b Garner                   | 9   |
| M Hendrick  | not out                    | 2   |
| Extras      | (19 b, 13 lb, 10 nb, 10 w) | 52  |
| Total       | (all out, 111.1 overs)     | 252 |

Fall of wickets:
1-46 (Gooch), 2-68 (Tavaré), 3-174 (Woolmer), 4-175 (Gower),
5-180 (Botham), 6-183 (Boycott), 7-218 (Knott), 8-237 (Willey),
9-248 (Willis), 10-252 (Lever, 111.1 ov)

## West Indies bowling

|           | Ovs  | Ms | Runs | Wkts |
|-----------|------|----|------|------|
| Roberts   | 24   | 6  | 57   | 3    |
| Holding   | 26   | 5  | 65   | 0    |
| Marshall  | 24   | 8  | 44   | 2    |
| Garner    | 34.1 | 20 | 30   | 4    |
| Greenidge | 3    | 2  | 4    | 0    |

## West Indies second innings

| CG Greenidge   | c Knott b Willis         | 6   |
|----------------|--------------------------|-----|
| DL Haynes      | run out                  | 62  |
| IVA Richards   | lbw b Botham             | 48  |
| SFAF Bacchus   | c Knott b Hendrick       | 19  |
| AI Kallicharran| c Knott b Willis         | 9   |
| *CH Lloyd      | lbw b Willis             | 3   |
| +DL Murray     | c Hendrick b Willis      | 16  |
| MD Marshall    | b Willis                 | 7   |
| AME Roberts    | not out                  | 22  |
| MA Holding     | not out                  | 0   |
| J Garner       |                          |     |
| Extras         | (8 lb, 9 nb)             | 17  |
| Total          | (8 wickets, 68.4 overs)  | 209 |

Fall of wickets:
1-11 (Greenidge), 2-69 (Richards), 3-109 (Bacchus), 4-125 (Kallicharran), 5-129 (Lloyd), 6-165 (Murray), 7-180 (Marshall), 8-205 (Haynes)

## England bowling

|          | Ovs  | Ms | Runs | Wkts |
|----------|------|----|------|------|
| Willis   | 26   | 4  | 65   | 5    |
| Lever    | 8    | 2  | 25   | 0    |
| Hendrick | 14   | 5  | 40   | 1    |
| Botham   | 16.4 | 6  | 48   | 1    |
| Gooch    | 2    | 1  | 2    | 0    |
| Willey   | 2    | 0  | 12   | 0    |

Unthinkably, the next four Tests all finished as draws, leaving the West Indies as series victors. Rain washed out much of the Lord's match, although Haynes, Richards and Gooch found time to score hundreds.

More wet weather disrupted the Old Trafford game, with Clive Lloyd scoring 101 on the ground where he played much of his county cricket. The next game, at the Kennington Oval, wasn't quite as memorable for the left-hander, with Lloyd pulling a muscle in the field and being unable to bat. Richards took over the captaincy and kept it for the final match of the rubber, another rain-ruined contest, at Leeds.

Garfield Sobers on his way to scoring 94 for Nottinghamshire against Derbyshire at Ilkeston in 1969. Bob Taylor is the wicketkeeper and Ian Buxton is the fielder. The ground proved to be a favourite for the left-hander. In 9 innings there he averaged 74.14 and won the Walter Lawrence Trophy in 1974 for a century in just 83 minutes, the fastest of the season.

Sobers in typical pose, hitting out at Trent Bridge.

Deryck Murray played in 97 first class matches for Notts between 1966 and 1969 as well as having a distinguished career behind the stumps for the West Indies.

Garfield Sobers strides out to bat alongside Mike Smedley at Trent Bridge. Smedley had the distinction of scoring two centuries against touring West Indian sides.

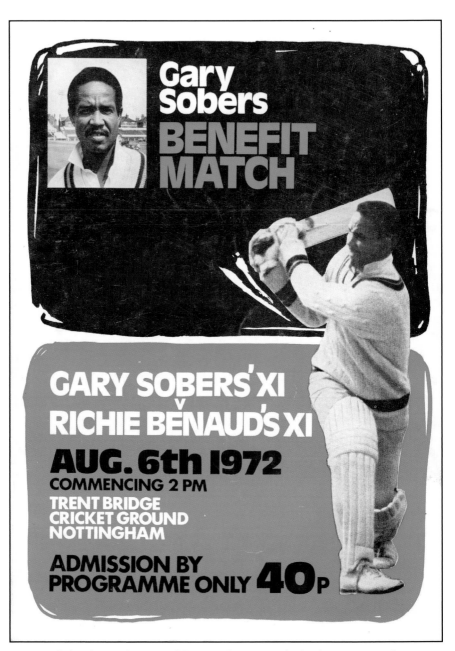

Sobers' contribution to Notts cricket was such that he was granted a Benefit Match during his fifth season with the club.

Sobers, as club captain, presents Derek Randall with his Notts Second XI cap, with Kevin Cooper and Dusty Hare next in line to receive theirs. Phillip Wilkinson is left of screen and Nirmal Nanan is in the centre of the photo.

In 1989 Garfield Sobers returned to Nottingham and met some of his former team-mates at a reunion dinner at the Commodore, Nottingham. Harry Latchman is on the back row next to Sobers, with Deryck Murray in the centre of the front row.

Franklyn Stephenson joined Nottinghamshire in 1988 and
performed the first class 'double' of 1,000 runs and 100 wickets.
A pose for the cameras to celebrate the achievement.

Above: Franklyn Stephenson recuperates whilst watching the England v West Indies Test match at Trent Bridge. A fortnight earlier he had sustained a broken nose when batting for Notts against the bowling of Gloucestershire's Kevin Curran. Attended by the club physio, Sheila Ball, the Barbadian allegedly asked for 'a plaster and a helmet' before resuming his innings.

Below: Upon arriving at Trent Bridge Franklyn met club skipper, Tim Robinson, plus Mick Newell, who seems to be commenting upon the height difference between the two.

Left: The 1988 Trent Bridge Test between England and the West Indies was drawn. Carl Hooper blazes through the off-side, watched by 'keeper Paul Downton.

Below: David Gower edges Curtly Ambrose into the safe gloves of Jeffrey Dujon.

The series began with good runs for Graham Gooch and Viv Richards
in Nottingham. The England opener made scores of 73 and 146
with the West Indies' captain making 80.

Sherwin Campbell clips to leg, with Jack Russell looking on,
England v West Indies at Trent Bridge 1995.

Above: A young Shivnarine Chanderpaul and Stuart Williams
take a well-deserved break during play.

Below: England's players gather on the Trent Bridge balcony at the end of the game.
Graeme Hick (far right) scored an unbeaten 118 in the first innings of the match.

Former Nottinghamshire player Jimmy Adams, skipper of the
West Indies on their 2000 tour of the UK.

Above: Vasbert Drakes spent the 1999 season with Nottinghamshire. Here he bowls in a pre-World Cup warm-up match against Sri Lanka at Trent Bridge.

Below: The West Indies defeated England by 93 runs in the 2007 Trent Bridge ODI – Dwayne Bravo enjoyed the moment.

Right: Daren Powell won the man of the match award after taking 4-40 in West Indies' 2007 Trent Bridge success over England. Here he celebrates the dismissal of Kevin Pietersen.

Below: The West Indies win – let the celebrations begin.

On Nottinghamshire's 2012 tour of Barbados, the players met two former county legends, Sir Garfield Sobers (above) and Franklyn Stephenson (below).

The three Barbadians who have played for Nottinghamshire, Vasbert Drakes, Sir Garfield Sobers and Franklyn Stephenson, together at the Kensington Oval, March 2012.

The Nottinghamshire squad in Barbados, 2012.

# Defeated at last

# 1984

The West Indies had retained their grip on the Wisden Trophy by defeating England in the Caribbean in early 1981. It was a series that began late after vandals damaged the Queen's Park Oval surface because of the omission of home favourite Deryck Murray, saw the second Test cancelled completely after the Guyanese authorities refused to let England's South African-born bowler Robin Jackman into the country and – sadly – was then overshadowed by the death of England's assistant manager and coach Ken Barrington, through a heart attack.

Victories in Trinidad and Barbados had given the home side the win in a series which also saw the Recreation Ground in Antigua christened as a Test venue with a century by Viv Richards.

Rebel West Indian tours to South Africa had ruled some leading players out of Test consideration since then, but it was still an immensely strong tour party that came to England in 1984. Again Lloyd was in charge, with Richards, Holding, Garner, Greenidge, Haynes and Marshall all still involved as his most experienced colleagues. Jeffrey Dujon of Jamaica had taken over as the regular wicket-keeper, whilst promising newcomers included the tall off-spinner Roger Harper.

For the first time, the summer schedule included an England versus West Indies One Day International at Trent Bridge. Later in the season, the tourists would return to Nottingham to face the county side in a three day match.

The opening four matches of the tour brought three wins, a draw and a stack of runs for Richards, Greenidge and Richie Richardson, ideal preparation ahead of the first ODI at Manchester. It is a good job that one of those mentioned had found some form because after 26 overs of the first international of the tour the West Indies were 102-7.

Richards appeared to be left high and dry as the rest of the top and middle order fell cheaply. Eldine Baptiste hung around for fifty minutes to make 26, but once he and Joel Garner had fallen, the score stood at 166-9. Last man Michael Holding made a dozen but he also had the best view in the ground to watch Richards at his imperious best. His innings of 189 not out was simply sensational and contained 21 x 4s and 5 x 6s and after an hour of mayhem the scoreboard looked much rosier at 272-9. Shell-shocked by the reversal in their fortunes, England were 8-2 after three overs and didn't recover, eventually being bowled out for just 168.

Just two days later the teams met again in Nottingham and a similar pattern emerged. Only this time Richards was also amongst the early West Indian casualties and only Lloyd's 52 saw them up to 179. It took England 47.5 overs to reach their victory target, with Andy Lloyd topping the scoring with 49, and the West Indies' unbeaten run at Trent Bridge ended in a three wicket defeat.

# England v West Indies

One Day International
2 June 1984
Toss: won by England, who elected to field
Umpires: HD Bird, DO Oslear

## Result: England won by 3 wickets

**West Indies innings**

| | | Runs | Balls | Mins | 4s | 6s | S-Rate |
|---|---|---|---|---|---|---|---|
| CG Greenidge | c Botham b Pringle | 20 | 38 | 53 | 2 | - | 52.63 |
| DL Haynes | lbw b Willis | 4 | 23 | 32 | - | - | 17.39 |
| RB Richardson | c Gower b Pringle | 10 | 30 | 28 | 1 | - | 33.33 |
| IVA Richards | c Pringle b Miller | 3 | 12 | 5 | - | - | 25.00 |
| HA Gomes | b Pringle | 15 | 39 | 44 | - | - | 38.46 |
| *CH Lloyd | c Pringle b Miller | 52 | 66 | 78 | 3 | 3 | 78.79 |
| +PJL Dujon | run out (Miller) | 21 | 36 | 59 | 1 | - | 58.33 |
| MD Marshall | run out (Bairstow) | 20 | 22 | 30 | 1 | - | 90.91 |
| EAE Baptiste | lbw b Willis | 19 | 16 | 28 | 1 | - | 118.75 |
| MA Holding | b Botham | 0 | 2 | 2 | - | - | 0.00 |
| J Garner | not out | 6 | 11 | 13 | - | - | 54.55 |
| Extras | (7 lb, 2 nb) | 9 | | | | | |
| Total | (all out, 48.3 ovs) | 179 | | | | | |

Fall of wickets:

1-24 (Haynes), 2-38 (Greenidge), 3-39 (Richardson), 4-43 (Richards), 5-75 (Gomes), 6-128 (Dujon), 7-148 (Lloyd), 8-160 (Marshall), 9-161 (Holding), 10-179 (Baptiste, 48.3 ov)

## England bowling

|         | Ovs  | Ms | Runs | Wkts | Ws | NBs | S-Rate | Econ |
|---------|------|----|------|------|----|-----|--------|------|
| Willis  | 9.3  | 0  | 26   | 2    | -  | -   | 28.50  | 2.74 |
| Botham  | 9    | 1  | 33   | 1    | -  | -   | 54.00  | 3.67 |
| Pringle | 10   | 3  | 21   | 3    | -  | -   | 20.00  | 2.10 |
| Miller  | 10   | 2  | 44   | 2    | -  | -   | 30.00  | 4.40 |
| Foster  | 10   | 0  | 46   | 0    | -  | -   | -      | 4.60 |

## England innings

|               |                        | Runs | Balls | Mins | 4s | 6s | S-Rate |
|---------------|------------------------|------|-------|------|----|----|--------|
| G Fowler      | b Baptiste             | 25   | 62    | 96   | 2  | -  | 40.32  |
| TA Lloyd      | c Dujon b Baptiste     | 49   | 103   | 117  | 1  | -  | 47.57  |
| *DI Gower     | lbw b Marshall         | 36   | 42    | 59   | 3  | -  | 85.71  |
| AJ Lamb       | b Gomes                | 11   | 24    | 24   | -  | -  | 45.83  |
| IT Botham     | c Gomes b Holding      | 15   | 23    | 45   | 1  | -  | 65.22  |
| MW Gatting    | b Garner               | 6    | 14    | 15   | -  | -  | 42.86  |
| +DL Bairstow  | b Holding              | 9    | 16    | 22   | -  | -  | 56.25  |
| G Miller      | not out                | 3    | 6     | 8    | -  | -  | 50.00  |
| DR Pringle    | not out                | 2    | 3     | 1    | -  | -  | 66.67  |
| NA Foster     |                        |      |       |      |    |    |        |
| RGD Willis    |                        |      |       |      |    |    |        |
| Extras        | (4 b, 14 lb, 6 nb)     | 24   |       |      |    |    |        |
| Total         | (7 wkts, 47.5 ovs)     | 180  |       |      |    |    |        |

Fall of wickets:

1-75 (Fowler), 2-103 (Lloyd), 3-131 (Lamb), 4-145 (Gower), 5-157 (Gatting), 6-173 (Botham), 7-177 (Bairstow)

**West Indies bowling**

|          | Ovs  | Ms | Runs | Wkts | Ws | NBs | S-Rate | Econ |
|----------|------|----|------|------|----|-----|--------|------|
| Garner   | 9    | 1  | 22   | 1    | -  | -   | 54.00  | 2.44 |
| Holding  | 8.5  | 1  | 29   | 2    | -  | -   | 26.50  | 3.28 |
| Marshall | 10   | 1  | 30   | 1    | -  | -   | 60.00  | 3.00 |
| Baptiste | 10   | 2  | 31   | 2    | -  | -   | 30.00  | 3.10 |
| Richards | 5    | 0  | 23   | 0    | -  | -   | -      | 4.60 |
| Gomes    | 5    | 0  | 21   | 1    | -  | -   | 30.00  | 4.20 |

West Indies won the third and final ODI by eight wickets at Lord's to take the series 2-1. Richards, with 84, and Larry Gomes, who made 56, shared in an unbroken third wicket stand of 134 to guide their side to a winning score of 197-2.

Turning their attentions from the one day game to the five day format, the West Indies then ruthlessly and efficiently won the opening Test match by an innings. Batting first England were quickly in disarray, losing Graham Fowler and Derek Randall for ducks and having debutant Andy Lloyd forced to retire hurt after being hit on the temple by Malcolm Marshall.

Randall had been dismissed by Joel Garner and he fell to the same bowler for a single in the second innings, bringing the Nottinghamshire man's Test career to an end after 47 appearances. One of the three changes for the Second Test saw Randall's new county team-mate Chris Broad earn his first selection. The left-handed opening batsman had moved to Trent Bridge from Gloucestershire during the previous winter.

Broad made 55 in his first Test innings, but his side still fell to a nine wicket defeat. The margin of victory is perhaps slightly exaggerated as they chased down 342 for the loss of only one wicket, thanks to a double hundred from Gordon Greenidge.

An eight wicket success at Leeds ensured the series would be won and further victories at Old Trafford and the Kennington Oval gave the West Indian side the distinction of becoming the first touring side to win all five Tests in an overseas series, prompting their jubilant supporters to coin the phrase ' blackwash'.

Between the final two matches in the series, the tourists had returned to Trent Bridge to face Nottinghamshire in a three-day first class fixture.

Clive Lloyd led a strong side, but it was one of his younger charges that made the most of ideal batting conditions on the opening day. Gus Logie, from Trinidad and Tobago, hadn't been able to force his way into the Test side that summer but had still put together an average of over 73 in the county games.

He would later make Test appearances at Trent Bridge during both of the next two tours, but in his first appearance at the ground he scored a classy 122 not out in 151 minutes, with sixteen boundaries. Earlier Desmond Haynes had made 69 and Vivian Richards 81, but Logie was nicely set at the close of the first day with his side on 361-4.

For the home side Kevin Cooper is worthy of mention. The seamer began the day with six consecutive maidens and was the stand-out performer with figures of 25-11-44-1. Sadly, for all concerned, heavy rain then set in and completely washed out days two and three.

*1, 2, 3 August 1984*
*West Indians 361-4 (Logie 122)*
*Notts did not bat*
*Match Drawn*

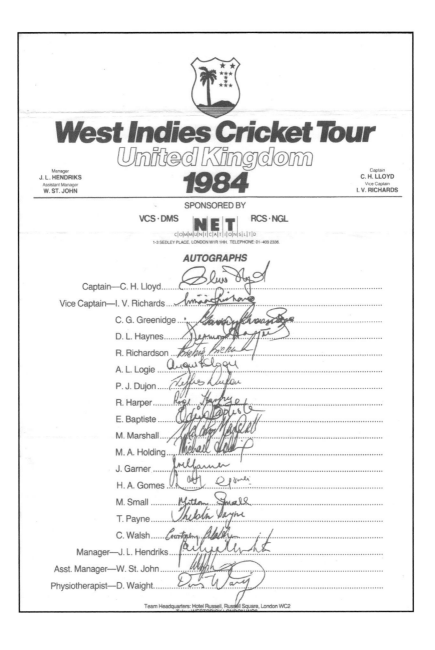

# Gooch saves England

# 1988

The West Indies arrived in the UK in 1988 having remained undefeated since their previous tour there four years earlier. During the interim period there had been several personnel changes, with Vivian Richards succeeding Clive Lloyd as captain and the retirements of both Michael Holding and Joel Garner.

Nevertheless, the wins had kept on coming – including a 3-1 success in Australia in 1984-5 – and then, a year later, a second consecutive 5-0 drubbing of England, this time in the Caribbean. Malcolm Marshall and Garner had taken 27 wickets apiece during that series and such was their dominance over England, none of David Gower's side registered a three figure score during the entire series.

By the time of the 1988 season, Mike Gatting had taken over the mantle as England captain and led his side to a morale-boosting series victory over the West Indies by winning all three One Day Internationals. Hopes were high that England would be able to end their sorry run of Test match defeats against the West Indies, which, as the sides headed for Trent Bridge for the first contest of the summer, stood at ten matches.

The opening day again showed England's frailties with the bat. Graham Gooch of Essex and Nottinghamshire's own Chris Broad put on 125 for the first wicket, but by stumps, after a compelling but fairly dour six hours, the score had slipped to 220-5, with Marshall taking four of the wickets to fall. Gooch had made 73 and Broad 54, in four hours, but Gatting, Gower and Lamb had all fallen cheaply. Apart from Pringle's 39 there wasn't much resistance thereafter, as Marshall finished with 6-69 and Curtly Ambrose mopped up the other four.

Rain and bad light frequently interrupted the West Indies, but despite regular stoppages they built a first innings lead of more than 200 before Richards declared late on the fourth evening.

The captain had made 80 out of a scorecard that featured many healthy contributions, with the top nine all getting into double figures. Carl Hooper hit 84, Malcolm Marshall 72 and Desmond Haynes 60.

A splendid century from Gooch, aided by an unbeaten 88 from Gower, took England to safety on the final day, ending that sorry run of defeats.

# England v West Indies

(The Trent Bridge Tests)
2, 3, 4, 6, 7 June 1988 (5-day match)
Toss: won by England who elected to bat
Umpires: HD Bird, J Birkenshaw

## Result: Match drawn

**England first innings**

| | | |
|---|---|---|
| GA Gooch | b Marshall | 73 |
| BC Broad | b Marshall | 54 |
| *MW Gatting | c Logie b Marshall | 5 |
| DI Gower | c Dujon b Ambrose | 18 |
| AJ Lamb | lbw b Marshall | 0 |
| DR Pringle | b Marshall | 39 |
| +PR Downton | not out | 16 |
| JE Emburey | c Dujon b Marshall | 0 |
| PAJ DeFreitas | b Ambrose | 3 |
| PW Jarvis | b Ambrose | 6 |
| GR Dilley | b Ambrose | 2 |
| Extras | (13 lb, 11 nb, 5 w) | 29 |
| Total | (all out, 101 overs) | 245 |

Fall of wickets:
1-125 (Gooch), 2-141 (Gatting), 3-161 (Broad), 4-161 (Lamb),
5-186 (Gower), 6-223 (Pringle), 7-223 (Emburey), 8-235
(DeFreitas), 9-243 (Jarvis), 10-245 (Dilley)

**West Indies bowling**

| | Ovs | Ms | Runs | Wkts |
|---|---|---|---|---|
| Marshall | 30 | 4 | 69 | 6 |
| Patterson | 16 | 2 | 49 | 0 |
| Ambrose | 26 | 10 | 53 | 4 |
| Walsh | 20 | 4 | 39 | 0 |
| Hooper | 8 | 1 | 20 | 0 |
| Richards | 1 | 0 | 2 | 0 |

## West Indies first innings

| | | |
|---|---|---|
| CG Greenidge | c Downton b Jarvis | 25 |
| DL Haynes | c Downton b Jarvis | 60 |
| RB Richardson | c Gatting b Emburey | 17 |
| *IVA Richards | c Gooch b DeFreitas | 80 |
| CL Hooper | c Downton b DeFreitas | 84 |
| AL Logie | c Gooch b Pringle | 20 |
| +PJL Dujon | c and b Dilley | 16 |
| MD Marshall | b Emburey | 72 |
| CEL Ambrose | run out | 43 |
| CA Walsh | not out | 3 |
| BP Patterson | | |
| Extras | (6 b, 8 lb, 14 nb) | 28 |
| Total | (9 wkts, dec., 129.1 ovs) | 448 |

Fall of wickets:
1-54 (Greenidge), 2-84 (Richardson), 3-159 (Haynes), 4-231 (Richards), 5-271 (Logie), 6-309 (Dujon), 7-334 (Hooper), 8-425 (Marshall), 9-448 (Ambrose)

### England bowling

| | Ovs | Ms | Runs | Wkts |
|---|---|---|---|---|
| Dilley | 34 | 5 | 101 | 1 |
| DeFreitas | 27 | 5 | 93 | 2 |
| Jarvis | 18.1 | 1 | 63 | 2 |
| Pringle | 34 | 11 | 82 | 1 |
| Emburey | 16 | 4 | 95 | 2 |

## England second innings

| | | |
|---|---|---|
| GA Gooch | c Dujon b Patterson | 146 |
| BC Broad | c Dujon b Ambrose | 16 |
| *MW Gatting | b Marshall | 29 |
| DI Gower | not out | 88 |
| AJ Lamb | not out | 6 |
| DR Pringle | | |
| +PR Downton | | |
| JE Emburey | | |
| PAJ DeFreitas | | |
| PW Jarvis | | |
| GR Dilley | | |
| Extras | (10 lb, 6 nb) | 16 |
| Total | (3 wkts., 108 overs) | 301 |

Fall of wickets:
1-39 (Broad), 2-116 (Gatting), 3-277 (Gooch)

### West Indies bowling

| | Ovs | Ms | Runs | Wkts |
|---|---|---|---|---|
| Marshall | 13 | 4 | 23 | 1 |
| Patterson | 24 | 6 | 69 | 1 |
| Ambrose | 23 | 4 | 56 | 1 |
| Walsh | 25 | 5 | 84 | 0 |
| Richards | 9 | 1 | 26 | 0 |
| Hooper | 14 | 1 | 33 | 0 |

In the aftermath of the Trent Bridge Test the media ran stories associating Mike Gatting with alleged scurrilous behaviour with a local barmaid. The incident was quickly acted upon by the selection panel who ousted the player and replaced him as captain by John Emburey.

The West Indies ensured it wouldn't be a happy rein for the Middlesex man by heavily defeating his side at both Lord's and Old Trafford. Emburey – and six other players – paid the price in a dramatic re-shuffle ahead of the Fourth Test at Leeds.

Another new captain was introduced, Kent's Chris Cowdrey – emulating his father, Colin, who had led his country against the West Indies in 1966. Despite all of the changes the outcome was all-too-familiar as England twice folded cheaply to lose by ten wickets.

A foot injury to Cowdrey ruled him out of the final match, meaning that a fourth skipper, Gooch, would be needed but an eight wicket defeat meant that the West Indies would take the series 4-0, having won 14 out of 15 matches against England.

With the series already in their pocket, the tourists had visited Trent Bridge in late July to face a Nottinghamshire side that included a new face amongst their ranks. 23 year old South African triallist Dave Callaghan – later to play ODI cricket for his country – made his debut in English cricket and leaving a lasting impression.

Apart from Callaghan, Notts included New Zealander Chris Cairns and Franklyn Stephenson from Barbados in their starting eleven.

Cairns removed both Jeff Dujon and Carl Hooper on the first morning but it the fall of the third wicket made the headlines and the Nottinghamshire record books. With his first delivery for the county, the medium paced Callaghan clean bowled Keith Arthurton – making him only the fourth bowler to achieve the feat for Notts (Steve Sylvester in 1994 became the fifth).

Captain Vivian Richards blasted a quickfire 75 and Gus Logie made 53 but the batting honours went to Gordon Greenidge who made 101.

Showers disrupted the second day but the county side did well to reach 247 on the third, after being 11-3 at one stage, after losing Mick Newell, Tim Robinson and Paul Johnson. An undefeated 63 from Chris Scott plus good runs from Stephenson, who made 59, John Birch 32 and Callaghan 29 ensured respectability and a drawn outcome.

There was only time for the West Indies to face two overs in their second innings, with John Birch bowling the first and 'keeper Scott the other – his bowling debut.

*27, 28, 29 July 1988*
*West Indians 362 (Greenidge 101, Cairns 4-82) and 17-0*
*Notts 247 (Scott 63 no, Stephenson 59)*

# FRANKLYN STEPHENSON

### *Date of birth: 8 April 1959 Saint James, Barbados*

Widely regarded as the best West Indian cricketer never to play a Test match, Franklyn Stephenson had a colourful career to say the least.

Between October 1981 and May 1982 he began his first class career in three different countries, playing for Tasmania, his native Barbados and then Gloucestershire.

A powerful right handed batsman and genuinely fast right arm bowler, he joined Lawrence Rowe and Alvin Kallicharran's rebel West Indian X1 that toured South Africa in 1982-83, immediately earning a lifetime ban from appearing for the recognised West Indies side. This ban was eventually lifted in 1992 but too late for 'Franky' to be considered.

In 1988 he joined Nottinghamshire and enjoyed the most sensational of debut seasons. Since the reduction of firs class games in 1969, only one player, the New Zealander Richard Hadlee – also with Notts, had achieved the legendary double of 1,000 runs and 100 wickets in first class cricket.

Franklyn's heroics saw him become the second player – and so far the last – to achieve the feat. Incredibly he got there by scoring a century in each innings of Nottinghamshire's final match of the season, against Yorkshire, as well as taking eleven wickets in the game.

Despite his own individual brilliance, somehow Notts still contrived to lose the game by 127 runs but his all-round genius saw him named as a Wisden Cricketer of the Year.

Renowned for becoming one of the first fast bowlers to develop a truly devilish slower delivery, he was an outstanding performer for Nottinghamshire.

Over a four year period for them Franklyn played 82 first class games, scoring 2845 runs and claiming 349 wickets at an average of 23.

After moving to Sussex in 1992 he spent a further four seasons in county cricket before ending his playing days back in South Africa.

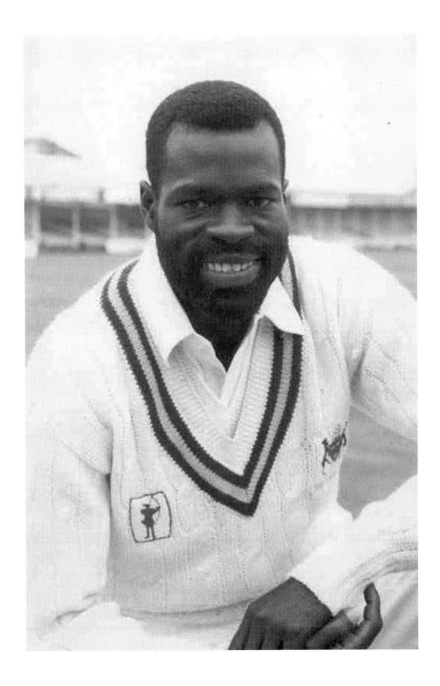

# Illy fairytale ends in defeat

# 1991

England's shocking run against the West Indies, which had stretched to fourteen defeats in fifteen matches, ended in Jamaica in early 1990 when Graham Gooch's side won by nine wickets in a match that marked the Test debuts of both Alec Stewart and Nasser Hussain.

A wash-out in Guyana and a draw in Trinidad followed, leaving England still 1-0 ahead going into the fourth game in Barbados. There, a devastating second innings performance from Curtly Ambrose, which produced figures of 8-45 – the best of his career – emphatically levelled matters ahead of the decider in Antigua.

Dismissed for just 260 England were already behind in that game before they'd managed to separate the openers. Greenidge – playing in his 100th Test – and Haynes put on 298, with both men making big centuries, the former 149 and his partner 167. With a lead of almost 200 the pace battery of the home side, led by Ambrose, Bishop and Walsh, blew England away to retain their grip on the Wisden Trophy.

A home series win over Australia had preceded the West Indies trip to the British Isles in 1991 and – as on their previous tour – they soon found themselves on the wrong end of a 3-0 scoreline in the ODIs.

England introduced five new players in those three matches: Graeme Hick, Mark Ramprakash, Richard Illingworth and Dermot Reeve, plus Gloucestershire's David Lawrence, who had one Test appearance to his name but had not played in an ODI before. Hick and Ramprakash impressed sufficiently to keep their place in the side for the start of the Test series, with Glamorgan seamer Steve Watkin also getting a debut in the opening match of the rubber at Leeds.

A second innings 154 not out from captain Gooch, who carried his bat in bowler-friendly conditions, paved the way for an England victory and an early series lead. Robin Smith, for England, and Carl Hooper for the tourists, both scored hundreds in the drawn Second Test at Lord's, so the sides headed for Nottingham with the hosts still 1-0 up.

Lawrence made the England starting eleven, as did Illingworth for his Test debut. The home side made exactly 300, with Gooch and Smith passing fifty and Ambrose getting a five-wicket haul. West Indies lost Haynes early and then Richard Illingworth bowled Phil Simmons, adding his name to the list of those that had taken a wicket with their first delivery in Test cricket, the seventh Englishman to achieve the feat and first at Trent Bridge. Richards, Logie and Marshall all passed fifty to give the West Indies a lead of 97, but with England only making 211 second time around, the series was levelled early on the last day.

# England v West Indies

(The Trent Bridge Tests)
4, 5, 6, 8, 9 July 1991 (5-day match)
Toss: won by England, who elected to bat
Umpires: JH Hampshire, MJ Kitchen

## Result: West Indies won by 9 wickets

### England first innings

| | | |
|---|---|---|
| *GA Gooch | lbw b Marshall | 68 |
| MA Atherton | lbw b Ambrose | 32 |
| GA Hick | c Dujon b Ambrose | 43 |
| AJ Lamb | lbw b Ambrose | 13 |
| MR Ramprakash | b Ambrose | 13 |
| RA Smith | not out | 64 |
| +RC Russell | c Logie b Allen | 3 |
| DR Pringle | c sub (CB Lambert) b Allen | 0 |

| PAJ DeFreitas | b Walsh | 8 |
| RK Illingworth | c Hooper b Ambrose | 13 |
| DV Lawrence | c Allen b Marshall | 4 |
| Extras | (17 lb, 21 nb, 1 w) | 39 |
| Total | (all out, 103.5 overs) | 300 |

Fall of wickets:
1-108 (Atherton), 2-113 (Gooch), 3-138 (Lamb), 4-186
(Ramprakash), 5-192 (Hick), 6-212 (Russell), 7-217 (Pringle), 8-228
(DeFreitas), 9-270 (Illingworth), 10-300 (Lawrence, 103.5 ov)

### West Indies bowling

| | Ovs | Ms | Runs | Wkts |
| --- | --- | --- | --- | --- |
| Ambrose | 34 | 7 | 74 | 5 |
| Marshall | 21.5 | 6 | 54 | 2 |
| Walsh | 24 | 4 | 75 | 1 |
| Allen | 17 | 0 | 69 | 2 |
| Hooper | 6 | 4 | 10 | 0 |
| Richards | 1 | 0 | 1 | 0 |

### West Indies first innings

| PV Simmons | b Illingworth | 12 |
| DL Haynes | c Smith b Lawrence | 18 |
| RB Richardson | b Lawrence | 43 |
| CL Hooper | c Russell b DeFreitas | 11 |
| *IVA Richards | b Illingworth | 80 |
| AL Logie | c Ramprakash b DeFreitas | 78 |
| +PJL Dujon | c Hick b Pringle | 19 |
| MD Marshall | c Illingworth b DeFreitas | 67 |
| CEL Ambrose | b Illingworth | 17 |
| CA Walsh | lbw b Pringle | 12 |
| IBA Allen | not out | 4 |
| Extras | (2 b, 13 lb, 20 nb, 1 w) | 36 |
| Total | (all out, 118.1 overs) | 397 |

Fall of wickets:
1-32 (Haynes), 2-32 (Simmons), 3-45 (Hooper), 4-118 (Richardson), 5-239 (Richards), 6-272 (Logie), 7-324 (Dujon), 8-358 (Ambrose), 9-392 (Walsh), 10-397 (Marshall, 118.1 ov)

## England bowling

|            | Ovs  | Ms | Runs | Wkts |
|------------|------|----|------|------|
| DeFreitas  | 31.1 | 9  | 67   | 3    |
| Lawrence   | 24   | 2  | 116  | 2    |
| Illingworth| 33   | 8  | 110  | 3    |
| Pringle    | 25   | 6  | 71   | 2    |
| Hick       | 5    | 0  | 18   | 0    |

## England second innings

| *GA Gooch      | b Ambrose             | 13  |
|----------------|-----------------------|-----|
| MA Atherton    | b Marshall            | 4   |
| GA Hick        | c Dujon b Ambrose     | 0   |
| AJ Lamb        | lbw b Marshall        | 29  |
| MR Ramprakash  | c Dujon b Ambrose     | 21  |
| RA Smith       | c Richards b Walsh    | 15  |
| +RC Russell    | b Walsh               | 3   |
| DR Pringle     | c Simmons b Walsh     | 3   |
| PAJ DeFreitas  | not out               | 55  |
| RK Illingworth | c Simmons b Walsh     | 13  |
| DV Lawrence    | c Hooper b Allen      | 34  |
| Extras         | (14 lb, 4 nb, 3 w)    | 21  |
| Total          | (all out, 79 overs)   | 211 |

Fall of wickets:
1-4 (Atherton), 2-8 (Hick), 3-25 (Gooch), 4-67 (Lamb), 5-100 (Smith), 6-106 (Ramprakash), 7-106 (Russell), 8-115 (Pringle), 9-153 (Illingworth), 10-211 (Lawrence, 79 ov)

**West Indies bowling**

|          | Ovs | Ms | Runs | Wkts |
|----------|-----|-----|------|------|
| Ambrose  | 27  | 7   | 61   | 3    |
| Marshall | 21  | 6   | 49   | 2    |
| Allen    | 7   | 2   | 23   | 1    |
| Walsh    | 24  | 7   | 64   | 4    |

**West Indies second innings**

| PV Simmons | c Russell b Lawrence | 1 |
|------------|---------------------|-----|
| DL Haynes | not out | 57 |
| RB Richardson | not out | 52 |
| CL Hooper | | |
| *IVA Richards | | |
| AL Logie | | |
| +PJL Dujon | | |
| MD Marshall | | |
| CEL Ambrose | | |
| CA Walsh | | |
| IBA Allen | | |
| Extras | (5 nb) | 5 |
| Total | (1 wkt., 32.2 overs) | 115 |

Fall of wickets:

1-1 (Simmons)

**England bowling**

|             | Ovs  | Ms | Runs | Wkts |
|-------------|------|-----|------|------|
| DeFreitas   | 11   | 3   | 29   | 0    |
| Lawrence    | 12.2 | 0   | 61   | 1    |
| Pringle     | 7    | 2   | 20   | 0    |
| Illingworth | 2    | 0   | 5    | 0    |

West Indies convincingly won the Fourth Test at Edgbaston, but, in a thrilling finale to the season, England bounced back to triumph at the Kennington Oval, with Phil Tufnell's 6-25 even forcing the tourists to follow-on in a match which also saw Ian Botham return to the team after a two year absence. The conclusion of the game – and the series – featured an emotional farewell to Viv Richards, playing his 121st and final Test.

# New young star

# THE NINETIES

England toured the Caribbean in early 1994, playing five One Day Internationals, which they took by three matches to two, and five Tests. Nottinghamshire's Chris Lewis made the travelling party, but it was Jamaica's Jimmy Adams, a couple of months before he was due to join the Trent Bridge staff, who took the Man of the Match honours after the West Indies won the opening Test. Adams' 95 not out was backed up by a brilliant fielding display, which produced six catches, and his slow left-arm also saw him amongst the wickets.

The same player scored 137 in the next match, in Guyana, but was outgunned by young star, Brian Lara, who hit 167 in an innings victory. With eleven wickets in the match, it was Curtly Ambrose who made the most telling contribution in Port-of-Spain, as the West Indies went 3-0 up, but the combined efforts of Alec Stewart – with centuries in both innings – and Angus Fraser, with 8-75 in the hosts' first knock, produced an England win in Bridgetown.

In cold isolation, the final match in Antigua was drawn. Dissecting the events though will reveal that Brian Lara smashed Sir Garfield Sobers' record for the highest Test score, which had stood since 1957. Lara, a 24-year-old left hander from Trinidad, batted for 766 minutes and hit 45 boundaries on his way to the new world record. Robin Smith and Michael Atherton both scored hundreds when England batted, but West Indies retained their hold on The Wisden Trophy and the Caribbean cricket followers had a new superstar to cherish.

West Indies came to the British Isles in 1995 on the back of their first series defeat in fifteen years, a 2-1 home loss to Australia. With Richie Richardson at the helm they didn't get off to the best of starts, losing to Hampshire and only drawing with Worcestershire and Somerset in their opening three warm-up fixtures.

The international programme began at Trent Bridge for the first of three One Day Internationals and Richardson invited England to bat first. Courtney Walsh soon picked off Michael Atherton at the start of an innings that brought him figures of 3-28 and the Man of the Match Award.

England only made 199, with Alec Stewart's 74 providing the bulk of the runs. West Indies were well on target when rain halted play after 19.5 overs with them on 76-1. If one more delivery had been bowled then the match would have been decided there and then. As it was, regulations allowed for a continuance into the second day and Sherwin Campbell's 80, plus 70 from Brian Lara, saw the visitors collect a five wicket victory with 14 deliveries to spare.

# JIMMY ADAMS

*Date of birth: 9 January 1968 Port Maria, St Mary, Jamaica*

Although he later played Minor Counties cricket for Berkshire, Jimmy Adams' only spell of county cricket came in 1994 when he spent a season at Trent Bridge.

Earlier in the same year the charismatic Jamaican had made five Test appearances in the Caribbean against England. A fortnight later he stepped off a plane and scored 117 not out at The Parks against Oxford University, not a bad way to mark your debut for a new side.

That summer the left hander scored 950 first class runs at an average of 35. He hit two further centuries, with a highest score of 144 not out against Somerset at Taunton. His slow left arm spin also produced 23 wickets at 31 apiece.

Jimmy would later go on to succeed Brian Lara as captain of his country, making a total of 54 Test appearances in all.

# England v West Indies

One Day International
Venue: Trent Bridge, Nottingham
24, 25 May 1995 (match carried over on to second day)
Toss: won by West Indies who elected to field
Umpires: NT Plews, DR Shepherd

## Result: West Indies won by 5 wickets

**England innings**

| | | Runs | Balls | Mins | 4s | 6s | S-Rate |
|---|---|---|---|---|---|---|---|
| *MA Atherton | c Lara b Walsh | 8 | 33 | 35 | - | - | 24.24 |
| +AJ Stewart | b Hooper | 74 | 127 | 157 | 11 | - | 58.27 |
| GA Hick | c Murray b Benjamin | 8 | 27 | 51 | - | - | 29.63 |
| GP Thorpe | c Murray b Walsh | 7 | 10 | 25 | - | - | 70.00 |
| NH Fairbrother | b Bishop | 12 | 23 | 30 | - | - | 52.17 |
| MR Ramprakash | b Walsh | 32 | 36 | 51 | 1 | 1 | 88.89 |
| PAJ DeFreitas | run out (Ambrose) | 15 | 29 | 23 | - | - | 51.72 |
| DG Cork | b Arthurton | 14 | 27 | 21 | - | - | 51.85 |
| D Gough | run out (Hooper) | 3 | 4 | 5 | - | - | 75.00 |
| SD Udal | not out | 5 | 7 | 9 | - | - | 71.43 |
| ARC Fraser | not out | 4 | 8 | 7 | - | - | 50.00 |
| Extras | (11 lb, 1 nb, 5 w) | 17 | | | | | |
| Total | (9 wkts., 55 ovs) | 199 | | | | | |

Fall of wickets:
1-25 (Atherton), 2-60 (Hick), 3-85 (Thorpe), 4-121 (Fairbrother), 5-125 (Stewart), 6-157 (DeFreitas), 7-186 (Ramprakash), 8-190 (Cork), 9-191 (Gough)

**West Indies bowling**

| | Ovs | Ms | Runs | Wkts | Ws | NBs | S-Rate | Econ |
|---|---|---|---|---|---|---|---|---|
| Ambrose | 8 | 1 | 33 | 0 | - | - | - | 4.12 |
| Walsh | 10 | 1 | 28 | 3 | - | - | 20.00 | 2.80 |
| Bishop | 11 | 2 | 30 | 1 | - | - | 66.00 | 2.73 |

| | | | | | | | |
|---|---|---|---|---|---|---|---|
| Benjamin | 8 | 1 | 22 | 1 | - | - | 48.00 | 2.75 |
| Hooper | 10 | 0 | 45 | 1 | - | - | 60.00 | 4.50 |
| Arthurton | 8 | 0 | 30 | 1 | - | - | 48.00 | 3.75 |

## West Indies innings

| | | Runs | Balls | Mins | 4s | 6s | S-Rate |
|---|---|---|---|---|---|---|---|
| CL Hooper | b Cork | 34 | 57 | 62 | 6 | - | 59.65 |
| SL Campbell | run out (Udal) | 80 | 137 | 193 | 8 | - | 58.39 |
| BC Lara | c Atherton b Gough | 70 | 95 | 100 | 7 | 1 | 73.68 |
| *RB Richardson | c DeFreitas b Gough | 1 | 7 | 7 | - | - | 14.29 |
| JC Adams | lbw b Cork | 2 | 12 | 12 | - | - | 16.67 |
| KLT Arthurton | not out | 1 | 3 | 10 | - | - | 33.33 |
| +JR Murray | not out | 7 | 6 | 4 | 1 | - | 116.67 |
| WKM Benjamin | | | | | | | |
| IR Bishop | | | | | | | |
| CEL Ambrose | | | | | | | |
| CA Walsh | | | | | | | |
| Extras | (1 lb, 1 nb, 4 w) | 6 | | | | | |
| Total | (5 wkts, 52.4 ovs) | 201 | | | | | |

Fall of wickets:

1-66 (Hooper), 2-180 (Lara), 3-183 (Richardson), 4-191 (Adams), 5-194 (Campbell)

## England bowling

| | Ovs | Ms | Runs | Wkts | Ws | NBs | S-Rate | Econ |
|---|---|---|---|---|---|---|---|---|
| DeFreitas | 10.4 | 1 | 44 | 0 | - | - | - | 4.12 |
| Fraser | 10 | 2 | 29 | 0 | - | - | - | 2.90 |
| Gough | 11 | 1 | 30 | 2 | - | - | 33.00 | 2.73 |
| Cork | 11 | 0 | 48 | 2 | - | - | 33.00 | 4.36 |
| Udal | 8 | 0 | 37 | 0 | - | - | - | 4.62 |
| Hick | 2 | 0 | 12 | 0 | - | - | - | 6.00 |

# CHRIS LEWIS

*Date of birth: 14 February 1968*
*Georgetown, Demerera, Guyana*

Chris Lewis was born in Guyana and played his early cricket there outside school hours. Moving to England at the age of 10, he was taught how to bowl properly and his skills developed rapidly.

A superb athlete, he entered county cricket with Leicestershire as a pacy right arm bowler and an aggressive lower order batsman. His county debut came in 1987 and by 1990 he'd earned a place on England's tour of the Caribbean but had to wait until July of that year before making his Test debut, against New Zealand.

Lewis joined Nottinghamshire for the start of the 1992 season, the first of three years in which he was at Notts. During that time he played in 37 first class fixtures, as well as continuing to appear in international cricket.

He twice scored double hundreds for Notts, against Durham in 1993 and Warwickshire a year later. The former innings was at Chester-le-Street and included a stand of 301 for the seventh wicket with Bruce French, a county record.

Lewis played his final match for Notts in September 1994, but his career then became shrouded in controversy. He joined Surrey and later Leicestershire again, and appeared in a total of 32 Test matches for England, but his career ended prematurely amidst his unsubstantiated claims that match-fixing was prevalent in the game.

In May 2009 Lewis was sentenced to 13 years in prison after being found guilty of smuggling cocaine into the country.

England recovered to win the next two matches to take a tight series, lifting expectations ahead of the six match Test series, the first time the two countries had contested one of that length.

Any notion that the West Indies may be a little vulnerable after their defeat to Australia was quickly dispelled as they won the opening Test at Leeds by nine wickets, with their battery of four fast bowlers, Ambrose, Walsh, Bishop and Kenny Benjamin, all impressing.

Derbyshire's Dominic Cork was given a debut at Lord's for the Second Test and he made a fairytale start by claiming 7-43 in the second innings to win the match for England and claim the Man of the Match award for himself.

Lancashire's Jason Gallian, later to play for Notts, made his first Test appearance in the third match at Edgbaston, although it was one to forget for England, who were on the wrong end of an innings defeat.

England levelled again by winning at Old Trafford. Brian Lara scored a majestic century, but the match was again swung by Cork – literally, as he found sufficient movement at the start of the fourth day to grab a first over hat-trick, removing Richie Richardson, Junior Murray and Carl Hooper to accelerate the West Indies' decline.

So, after four positive results had brought the series level at 2-2, the sides moved to Nottingham for the Fifth Test. Both sides made over 400 in the first innings. Batting first, England saw both Michael Atherton and Graeme Hick score hundreds, but Lara, in peak form, scored 152 from 182 deliveries.

England's second innings closed on 269-9 declared on the last day, but the West Indies missed a golden chance to win the game when Sherwin Campbell put down a routine two-handed offering at mid-wicket to dismiss Mike Watkinson. The Lancashire all-rounder was on 22 at the time and went on to make an unlikely 82 not out, sharing an unbroken stand of 80 with Richard Illingworth, batting heroically with a broken right index finger.

Trent Bridge groundsman Ron Allsopp – in the season of his retirement – had produced a very decent surface for batting and both sides made the most of it, despite the heroics of Kenny Benjamin, who took five wickets in each innings, to get ten in a match for the first time.

# England v West Indies

(The Trent Bridge Tests)
10, 11, 12, 13, 14 August 1995 (5-day match)
Toss: won by England who elected to bat
Umpires: CJ Mitchley, NT Plews

## Result: Match drawn

**England first innings**

| | | |
|---|---|---|
| NV Knight | lbw b Benjamin | 57 |
| *MA Atherton | run out | 113 |
| JP Crawley | c Williams b Benjamin | 14 |
| GP Thorpe | c Browne b Bishop | 19 |
| RK Illingworth | retired hurt | 8 |
| GA Hick | not out | 118 |
| C White | c Browne b Bishop | 1 |
| +RC Russell | c Browne b Bishop | 35 |
| M Watkinson | lbw b Benjamin | 24 |
| DG Cork | c Browne b Benjamin | 31 |
| ARC Fraser | b Benjamin | 0 |
| Extras | (4 b, 8 lb, 8 nb) | 20 |
| Total | (all out, 152.4 overs) | 440 |

Fall of wickets:
1-148 (Knight), 2-179 (Crawley), 3-206 (Atherton), 4-211 (Thorpe), 5-239 (White), 6-323 (Russell), 7-380 (Watkinson), 8-440 (Cork), 9-440 (Fraser, 152.4 ov)

## West Indies bowling

|           | Ovs  | Ms | Runs | Wkts |
|-----------|------|----|------|------|
| Walsh     | 39   | 5  | 93   | 0    |
| Bishop    | 30.1 | 6  | 62   | 3    |
| Benjamin  | 34.3 | 7  | 105  | 5    |
| Dhanraj   | 40   | 7  | 137  | 0    |
| Arthurton | 9    | 0  | 31   | 0    |

## West Indies first innings

| SC Williams     | c Atherton b Illingworth   | 62  |
|-----------------|----------------------------|-----|
| SL Campbell     | c Crawley b Watkinson      | 47  |
| BC Lara         | c Russell b Cork           | 152 |
| *RB Richardson  | c Hick b Illingworth       | 40  |
| KLT Arthurton   | b Illingworth              | 13  |
| R Dhanraj       | c Knight b Cork            | 3   |
| S Chanderpaul   | c Crawley b Watkinson      | 18  |
| +CO Browne      | st Russell b Illingworth   | 34  |
| IR Bishop       | c Hick b Watkinson         | 4   |
| KCG Benjamin    | not out                    | 14  |
| CA Walsh        | b Fraser                   | 19  |
| Extras          | (2 b, 7 lb, 2 nb)          | 11  |
| Total           | (all out, 148.3 overs)     | 417 |

Fall of wickets:
1-77 (Williams), 2-217 (Campbell), 3-273 (Richardson), 4-319 (Arthurton), 5-323 (Lara), 6-338 (Dhanraj), 7-366 (Chanderpaul), 8-374 (Bishop), 9-384 (Browne), 10-417 (Walsh, 148.3 ov)

## England bowling

|  | Ovs | Ms | Runs | Wkts |
|---|---|---|---|---|
| Fraser | 17.3 | 6 | 77 | 1 |
| Cork | 36 | 9 | 110 | 2 |
| Watkinson | 35 | 12 | 84 | 3 |
| Illingworth | 51 | 21 | 96 | 4 |
| Hick | 4 | 1 | 11 | 0 |
| White | 5 | 0 | 30 | 0 |

## England second innings

| *MA Atherton | c Browne b Bishop | 43 |
|---|---|---|
| JP Crawley | b Walsh | 11 |
| GA Hick | b Benjamin | 7 |
| GP Thorpe | c Browne b Walsh | 76 |
| C White | c Campbell b Bishop | 1 |
| +RC Russell | c Browne b Benjamin | 7 |
| NV Knight | c Browne b Benjamin | 2 |
| M Watkinson | not out | 82 |
| DG Cork | c Browne b Benjamin | 4 |
| ARC Fraser | c Arthurton b Benjamin | 4 |
| RK Illingworth | not out | 14 |
| Extras | (4 lb, 14 nb) | 18 |
| Total | (9 wkts, dec., 104 ovs) | 269 |

Fall of wickets:
1-17 (Crawley), 2-36 (Hick), 3-117 (Atherton), 4-125 (White), 5-139 (Russell), 6-148 (Knight), 7-171 (Thorpe), 8-176 (Cork), 9-189 (Fraser)

## West Indies bowling

|  | Ovs | Ms | Runs | Wkts |
|---|---|---|---|---|
| Walsh | 30 | 6 | 70 | 2 |
| Bishop | 21 | 8 | 50 | 2 |
| Benjamin | 25 | 8 | 69 | 5 |
| Dhanraj | 15 | 1 | 54 | 0 |
| Arthurton | 13 | 3 | 22 | 0 |

**West Indies second innings**

| | | |
|---|---|---:|
| BC Lara | c Russell b Fraser | 20 |
| SL Campbell | c Russell b Cork | 16 |
| S Chanderpaul | not out | 5 |
| +CO Browne | not out | 1 |
| SC Williams | | |
| *RB Richardson | | |
| KLT Arthurton | | |
| R Dhanraj | | |
| IR Bishop | | |
| KCG Benjamin | | |
| CA Walsh | | |
| Extras | | 0 |
| Total | (2 wkts.., 11 overs) | 42 |

**England bowling**

| | Ovs | Ms | Runs | Wkts |
|---|---|---|---|---|
| Fraser | 6 | 1 | 17 | 1 |
| Cork | 5 | 1 | 25 | 1 |

The sixth and final match of the rubber was seen as something of an anti-climax. Tickets had been sold out for the Kennington Oval match for many months and the exciting manner in which the series had gone to and fro had ensured it was all set up for a sensational decider. As it was, bat triumphed over ball again and a second consecutive draw was the outcome, meaning the West Indies clung on to The Wisden Trophy, which they'd won in 1973 and held for the next 22 years and 12 series.

England batted for most of the first two days, making 454, but that total was put in context by the West Indies reply. Their score of 692-8 declared was their highest against England and featured some outstanding strokeplay. Lara again led the way, making 179 – his third century in three matches – taking his series aggregate to 765. He was by no means alone though. Carl Hooper scored 127, Richie Richardson 93, Sherwin Campbell 89 and Shivnarine Chanderpaul 80. England had to bat out the final day, which they accomplished chiefly due to 95 from Atherton.

# HOME DOMINANCE

The opening Test match of England's 1998 tour of the West Indies ended after just 56 minutes of action at Sabina Park, Kingston. During that period a succession of batsmen had been hit as the tourists slumped to 17-3. After discussion, the surface was deemed unfit, the match abandoned as a draw and a sixth match was hastily added to the schedule.

Angus Fraser, who had enjoyed his previous tour to the region, took 8-53 in West Indies' first innings at Port-of-Spain, but an undefeated 94 from Guyana's Carl Hooper saw his side go ahead in the series. England levelled, on the same ground, but then lost heavily in Georgetown before drawing the penultimate match.

With the home nation 2-1 up, they headed to Antigua, where Lara won an important toss and fielded. His quick bowlers ran through England for 127 – a poor score that was put into context when the West Indies replied with 500-7 declared. Centuries from Hooper and Lambert, plus 92 from Wallace and 89 from the captain gave the home side a healthy lead and the springboard for an innings success.

# VASBERT DRAKES

*Date of birth: 5 August 1969 Springhead, St Andrew, Barbados*

Vasbert Drakes spent just the one season with Nottinghamshire, but he certainly made his mark during that 1999 campaign. Quick enough to be labelled a genuine fast bowler, he arrived at Trent Bridge having been ignored by the West Indies selectors since appearing in five One Day internationals against Australia in 1995.

He had previously played two seasons of county cricket for Sussex and then had three winters with Boland in South Africa, thereby ruling himself out of international recognition as he didn't meet the selection criteria by not playing in the West Indies' domestic tournaments.

Enlisted to spearhead the Notts bowling attack, he made his championship debut for Jason Gallian's side at Grace Road, Leicester and didn't have to bowl a single ball in the contest, as three of the four days were lost to rain.

Celebrated as a potential match-winner in limited overs cricket, his most startling performance for Notts came in a contest that had been virtually conceded. Playing against Derbyshire at Trent Bridge, the home side had mustered 269-7. Nevertheless, it didn't look like being enough as the visitors began the final over on 260-5, requiring just ten runs to win.

To everyone's sheer astonishment Vasbert then produced a once-in-a-lifetime finish. He yorked Phil De Freitas with the first ball of the over and then removed Adrian Rollins' middle stump with the next. He needed the assistance of the umpire to get his hat-trick – James Pyemont palpably out lbw – and then, for good measure, a full length delivery took out the leg stump of Simon Lacey.

Four wickets in four balls – the only time it has happened for a Nottinghamshire bowler in the shortened format of the game. A dot ball and a single ended the over by the way, enabling Notts to defeat their closest rivals in the most dramatic of fashions.

Vasbert later played for Warwickshire and Leicestershire, as well as winning a dozen Test caps for the West Indies.

He also features in Wisden as one of only four batsmen to have ever been given 'Timed Out'. Scheduled to appear for Border against Free State in September 2002 his flight was delayed by several hours and he didn't arrive in time to bat in the first innings of the game.

# The New Millenium

# 2000

West Indies shared the summer of 2000 with Zimbabwe, who also toured England. The three nations met in a triangular one day tournament and each played separate Test series against the hosts.

Trent Bridge staged a Test versus Zimbabwe that year and also an ODI against the West Indies. That match came midway through the summer and also midway through the Test programme, with West Indies, led by Jimmy Adams, winning at Edgbaston and losing the next at Lord's.

There was a familiar name to Nottinghamshire supporters when the home selectors announced their squad for the one day matches. Paul Franks, a 21-year-old all-rounder – although bowling was his stronger suit – sat and watched the first few matches before being given his chance on his home ground on 20 July 2000. He made an early impression, although didn't pick up a wicket, as England bowled first and limited the tourists to 195-9, a challenging if not daunting total from 50 overs.

Openers Marcus Trescothick and Alec Stewart put their side on the way to victory with a stand of 46, but once it had been broken with the loss of the Somerset man, no-one else could offer any support to Stewart. As it was, they still only needed five runs from the final over, with three wickets left and Stewart still there, unbeaten on 100.

Tragically, he couldn't get back on strike. Franks was run out for 4, and then Darren Gough and Alan Mullally both fell for second ball ducks to bowler Chris Gayle, who collected the Man of the Match Award as his side squeaked home by three runs in a real Trent Bridge thriller.

# England v West Indies

Nat West Bank Series 2000
Trent Bridge, Nottingham
20 July, 2000
Toss: won by England, who decided to field
Umpires: MJ Kitchen, B Leadbeater

## Result: West Indies won by 3 runs

**West Indies innings**

|  |  | Runs | Balls | Mins | 4s | 6s | S-Rate |
|---|---|---|---|---|---|---|---|
| SL Campbell | b Gough | 12 | 20 | 28 | 2 | - | 60.00 |
| CH Gayle | c White b Ealham | 37 | 71 | 80 | 4 | - | 52.11 |
| WW Hinds | c Hussain b Ealham | 10 | 32 | 41 | 2 | - | 31.25 |
| *JC Adams | b Mullally | 36 | 59 | 93 | 4 | - | 61.02 |
| RR Sarwan | b White | 20 | 36 | 40 | 1 | - | 55.56 |
| RL Powell | b White | 1 | 4 | 8 | - | - | 25.00 |
| +RD Jacobs | run out | 5 | 18 | 25 | - | - | 27.78 |
| MV Nagamootoo | c Ealham b Gough | 11 | 25 | 36 | - | - | 44.00 |
| FA Rose | c Franks b White | 29 | 26 | 41 | 3 | - | 111.54 |
| M Dillon | not out | 14 | 15 | 17 | 2 | - | 93.33 |
| RD King | not out | 1 | 2 | 3 | - | - | 50.00 |
| Extras | (2 b, 4 lb, 8 nb, 5 w) | 19 | | | | | |
| Total | (9 wkts, 50 ovs) | 195 | | | | | |

Fall of wickets:

1-34 (Campbell, 7.3 ov), 2-63 (Hinds, 17.6 ov), 3-70 (Gayle, 19.6 ov), 4-101 (Sarwan, 30.2 ov), 5-107 (Powell, 32.1 ov), 6-132 (Jacobs, 37.3 ov), 7-139 (Adams, 38.6 ov), 8-170 (Nagamootoo, 46.1 ov), 9-189 (Rose, 49.1 ov)

**England bowling**

|  | Ovs | Ms | Runs | Wkts | Ws | NBs | S-Rate | Econ |
|---|---|---|---|---|---|---|---|---|
| Franks | 9 | 0 | 48 | 0 | 1 | 5 | - | 5.33 |
| Gough | 10 | 0 | 34 | 2 | 2 | 2 | 30.00 | 3.40 |

| | | | | | | | | |
|---|---|---|---|---|---|---|---|---|
| Mullally | 10 | 0 | 29 | 1 | 1 | 1 | 60.00 | 2.90 |
| Ealham | 10 | 0 | 37 | 2 | - | - | 30.00 | 3.70 |
| White | 10 | 0 | 35 | 3 | 1 | - | 20.00 | 3.50 |
| Hick | 1 | 0 | 6 | 0 | - | - | - | 6.00 |

## England innings

| | | Runs | Balls | Mins | 4s | 6s | S-Rate |
|---|---|---|---|---|---|---|---|
| ME Trescothick | c Jacobs b King | 23 | 36 | 45 | 5 | - | 63.89 |
| +AJ Stewart | not out | 100 | 147 | 222 | 11 | - | 68.03 |
| A Flintoff | c Jacobs b King | 2 | 7 | 10 | - | - | 28.57 |
| GA Hick | b King | 0 | 1 | 1 | - | - | 0.00 |
| GP Thorpe | run out | 5 | 6 | 13 | - | - | 83.33 |
| *N Hussain | c Jacobs b Nagamootoo | 3 | 13 | 21 | - | - | 23.08 |
| C White | run out | 19 | 44 | 56 | - | - | 43.18 |
| MA Ealham | c Gayle b Rose | 16 | 32 | 37 | 2 | - | 50.00 |
| PJ Franks | run out | 4 | 17 | 26 | - | - | 23.53 |
| D Gough | b Gayle | 0 | 1 | 2 | - | - | 0.00 |
| AD Mullally | lbw b Gayle | 0 | 2 | 2 | - | - | 0.00 |
| Extras | (6 lb, 7 nb, 7 w) | 20 | | | | | |
| Total | (all out, 49.5 overs) | 192 | | | | | |

Fall of wickets:
1-46 (Trescothick, 10.4 ov), 2-49 (Flintoff, 12.5 ov), 3-49 (Hick, 12.6 ov),
4-56 (Thorpe, 15.4 ov), 5-75 (Hussain, 21.5 ov), 6-138 (White, 37.4 ov),
7-170 (Ealham, 44.5 ov), 8-191 (Franks, 49.1 ov), 9-192 (Gough, 49.3 ov),
10-192 (Mullally, 49.5 ov)

## West Indies bowling

| | Ovs | Ms | Runs | Wkts | Ws | NBs | S-Rate | Econ |
|---|---|---|---|---|---|---|---|---|
| King | 10 | 1 | 30 | 3 | 2 | - | 20.00 | 3.00 |
| Dillon | 10 | 1 | 52 | 0 | 3 | 4 | - | 5.20 |
| Rose | 10 | 0 | 31 | 1 | - | 2 | 60.00 | 3.10 |
| Nagamootoo | 10 | 1 | 41 | 1 | - | - | 60.00 | 4.10 |
| Gayle | 6.5 | 0 | 21 | 2 | - | - | 20.50 | 3.07 |
| Adams | 3 | 0 | 11 | 0 | 2 | 1 | - | 3.67 |

The Test series resumed with a draw at Old Trafford, which was then followed by an extraordinary outcome at Leeds, where England won by an innings inside two days after Andy Caddick had claimed four wickets in an over. Ambrose also collected his 400th wicket at this level during the England innings.

West Indies' grip on The Wisden Trophy was finally relinquished with a defeat at the Kennington Oval, ending a run of 31 years without losing a rubber to England.

# 2004

2004 saw back-to-back series being contested between England and the West Indies, beginning with four Tests in the Caribbean.

Once again Sabina Park was entrusted with the opening match, much to the delight of Steve Harmison. The tall Durham fast bowler made the most of the helpful conditions to inflict some of their own medicine upon the West Indies, who had been so used to dishing it out themselves over the previous 30 years. Harmison's second innings figures were 12.3-8-12-7 as the home side were dismissed for just 47 in only two hours.

The tone of the series set, England also won in Port-of-Spain and Bridgetown to take an unbeatable 3-0 lead, meaning there was little to play for but pride for the home nation in Antigua. Nottinghamshire's Chris Read had played in the three winning matches but was stood down for the match at the Recreation Ground, allowing Kent's Geraint Jones to make his England debut.

Ten years earlier Lara's 375 not out had broken the world record for the highest individual score in a Test match. That record had stood until October 2003, when Australia's Matthew Hayden made 380 for Australia against Zimbabwe at Perth. Returning to the 'Rec' in St John's, Antigua, Lara was all too aware of the region's disappointment at his side's performances against England. Winning the toss, he soon had the opportunity to dictate matters and was unbeaten on 86 out of a score of 208-2 on a rain-interrupted first day.

Resuming the next day, the little left hander, passed 100, 200 and 300 as stumps were reached at 595-5. On the third morning he regained the record and went on to reach exactly 400 before declaring the innings closed on a mammoth 751-5. The match was eventually drawn, but Lara's innings had again lifted home spirits and elevated 'The Prince of Trinidad' back to the top of the world stage.

Following on from the Tests a one day series finished 2-2, with three other matches washed out. Just a month later the West Indies began their tour of the UK and 'warmed-up' for a triangular one day series against the hosts and New Zealand with victories over Sussex and Kent.

Rain prevented a finish to their opening match against the Kiwis at Edgbaston, from where they moved to Trent Bridge to face England. Lara put England in to bat and immediately saw the decision vindicated as Ian Bradshaw, a medium-fast bowler from Barbados, sent back Trescothick and Vaughan inside the opening three overs. Jones and Strauss lifted England to 84-2, but from there they collapsed spectacularly, to be all out for just 147.

Chris Gayle had bowled the decisive final over of the match in the West Indies' win on their previous visit to Trent Bridge in 2000. This time, with a fluent 60 not out he eased his side to a comfortable seven wicket victory, although the Man-of-the-Match Award went to Dwayne Bravo for his 3-26, which helped blow away the England middle order.

# England v West Indies

Nat West Bank Series 2004
Trent Bridge, Nottingham
27 June, 2004
Toss: won by West Indies who decided to field
Umpires: MR Benson, DL Harper

## Result: West Indies won by 7 wickets

**England innings**

| | | Runs | Balls | Mins | 4s | 6s | S-Rate |
|---|---|---|---|---|---|---|---|
| ME Trescothick | c Lara b Bradshaw | 0 | 4 | 2 | - | - | 0.00 |
| *MP Vaughan | c Sarwan b Bradshaw | 1 | 6 | 11 | - | - | 16.67 |
| +GO Jones | b Rampaul | 35 | 45 | 79 | 7 | - | 77.78 |
| AJ Strauss | c Jacobs b Bravo | 43 | 63 | 94 | 6 | - | 68.25 |
| PD Collingwood | c Jacobs b Rampaul | 5 | 13 | 17 | - | - | 38.46 |
| A McGrath | c Gayle b Bravo | 9 | 16 | 22 | 1 | - | 56.25 |
| ID Blackwell | c Chanderpaul b Bravo | 4 | 7 | 10 | 1 | - | 57.14 |
| R Clarke | lbw b Smith | 11 | 31 | 60 | - | - | 35.48 |
| D Gough | b Lawson | 13 | 41 | 39 | 1 | - | 31.71 |
| SJ Harmison | b Lawson | 2 | 4 | 4 | - | - | 50.00 |
| JM Anderso n | not out | 2 | 5 | 4 | - | - | 40.00 |
| Extras (4 b, 5 lb, 5 nb, 8 w) | | 22 | | | | | |
| Total (all out, 38.2 overs) | | 147 | | | | | |

Fall of wickets:

1-0 (Trescothick, 0.4 ov), 2-2 (Vaughan, 2.1 ov), 3-84 (Jones, 16.5 ov), 4-102 (Collingwood, 20.6 ov), 5-104 (Strauss, 21.5 ov), 6-115 (Blackwell, 23.6 ov), 7-118 (McGrath, 25.2 ov), 8-139 (Gough, 35.5 ov), 9-145 (Harmison, 37.1 ov), 10-147 (Clarke, 38.2 ov)

## West Indies bowling

|  | Ovs | Ms | Runs | Wkts | Ws | NBs | S-Rate | Econ |
|---|---|---|---|---|---|---|---|---|
| Bradshaw | 10 | 3 | 32 | 2 | 3 | - | 30.00 | 3.20 |
| Lawson | 9 | 1 | 36 | 2 | - | 3 | 27.00 | 4.00 |
| Bravo | 10 | 2 | 26 | 3 | 2 | - | 20.00 | 2.60 |
| Rampaul | 6 | 0 | 34 | 2 | 3 | 2 | 18.00 | 5.67 |
| Smith | 3.2 | 1 | 10 | 1 | - | - | 20.00 | 3.00 |

## West Indies innings

|  |  | Runs | Balls | Mins | 4s | 6s | S-Rate |
|---|---|---|---|---|---|---|---|
| CH Gayle | not out | 60 | 90 | 147 | 9 | - | 66.67 |
| S Chanderpaul | b McGrath | 20 | 54 | 85 | 2 | - | 37.04 |
| DR Smith | c Trescothick b Anderson | 6 | 9 | 9 | 1 | - | 66.67 |
| RR Sarwan | c Trescothick b Anderson | 13 | 12 | 15 | 2 | - | 108.33 |
| *BC Lara | not out | 32 | 29 | 31 | 6 | - | 110.34 |
| RL Powell |  |  |  |  |  |  |  |
| DJ Bravo |  |  |  |  |  |  |  |
| +RD Jacobs |  |  |  |  |  |  |  |
| IDR Bradshaw |  |  |  |  |  |  |  |
| R Rampaul |  |  |  |  |  |  |  |
| JJC Lawson |  |  |  |  |  |  |  |
| Extras(4 lb, 13 w) |  | 17 |  |  |  |  |  |
| Total (3 wkts., 32.2 ovs) |  | 148 |  |  |  |  |  |

Fall of wickets:

1-62 (Chanderpaul, 19.2 ov), 2-71 (Smith, 20.6 ov), 3-93 (Sarwan, 24.5 ov)

## England bowling

|  | Ovs | Ms | Runs | Wkts | Ws | NBs | S-Rate | Econ |
|---|---|---|---|---|---|---|---|---|
| Gough | 9 | 0 | 33 | 0 | 3 | - | - | 3.67 |
| Harmison | 10 | 2 | 29 | 0 | 3 | - | - | 2.90 |
| Anderson | 7.2 | 0 | 39 | 2 | 6 | - | 22.00 | 5.32 |
| Clarke | 4 | 0 | 30 | 0 | - | - | - | 7.50 |
| McGrath | 2 | 0 | 13 | 1 | 1 | - | 12.00 | 6.50 |

Their win in Nottingham helped the West Indies qualify for the Final of the event at England's expense, but they then lost to New Zealand at Lord's.

With attention then switching back to five day cricket, England were emphatic winners of the opening Test, also at Lord's. A double hundred from Robert Key, centuries in both innings from Michael Vaughan and a further ton from Andrew Strauss were too much for the visitors, although Shiv Chanderpaul enjoyed a fine individual match, scoring 128 not out and 97 not out.

Flintoff and Trescothick for England and Sarwan for the West Indies scored hundreds at Edgbaston – where again it was all too easy for Vaughan's side, who then went on to take the series 4-0, with further triumphs at Old Trafford and the Oval.

# Promising
# youngsters

During the first decade of the 21st century, Nottinghamshire twice played host to West Indies' A sides in first class friendlies. In 2002 Wayne Noon skippered a Notts side that contained three debutants, Vikram Atri, Samit Patel and Will Smith.

The visiting side was captained by Daren Ganga, later to captain the West Indies in Test cricket, and also included nine others – with 'keeper Keith Hibbert the exception – who would play the game at the highest level over the next few years.

Atri made 98 in his first innings for the county, with the two other new boys both acquitting themselves well also. Ryan Hinds was the pick of the West Indian batsmen, but the possibility of a final day run chase being set up was washed away by bad weather.

# Nottinghamshire v West Indies 'A'

Trent Bridge
3rd, 4th, 5th July 2002 (3-day match)
Toss: won by Nottinghamshire, who elected to bat
Umpires: M Dixon, R Palmer

## Result: Match drawn

### Nottinghamshire first innings

| GE Welton | b Best | 43 |
|---|---|---|
| V Atri | c Morton b Hinds | 98 |
| BM Shafayat | lbw b Lawson | 27 |
| KP Pietersen | b Lawson | 1 |
| SR Patel | c Bravo b Best | 35 |
| WR Smith | not out | 38 |
| GD Clough | b Hinds | 5 |
| *+WM Noon | lbw b Lawson | 15 |
| TE Savill | b Lawson | 0 |
| PJ McMahon | lbw b Hinds | 0 |
| MN Malik | | |
| Extras | (6 b, 5 lb, 14 nb) | 25 |
| Total | (9 wkts. dec., 76.3 ovs) | 287 |

Fall of wickets:

1-55 (Welton), 2-117 (Shafayat), 3-119 (Pietersen), 4-213 (Patel), 5-229 (Atri), 6-241 (Clough), 7-284 (Noon), 8-284 (Savill), 9-287 (McMahon)

### West Indies A bowling

|        | Ovs  | Ms | Runs | Wkts |
|--------|------|----|------|------|
| Black  | 17   | 2  | 62   | 0    |
| Best   | 21   | 7  | 69   | 2    |
| Lawson | 20   | 1  | 91   | 4    |
| Hinds  | 18.3 | 1  | 54   | 3    |

### West Indies A first innings

| *D Ganga     | c Noon b Savill          | 10  |
|--------------|--------------------------|-----|
| DJ Pagon     | lbw b Savill             | 1   |
| DS Smith     | c Atri b Malik           | 31  |
| RS Morton    | c Atri b Clough          | 33  |
| RO Hinds     | c Shafayat b Clough      | 73  |
| DJ Bravo     | b Malik                  | 21  |
| LMP Simmons  | not out                  | 20  |
| +KH Hibbert  | b McMahon                | 6   |
| MI Black     | lbw b McMahon            | 8   |
| TL Best      |                          |     |
| JJC Lawson   |                          |     |
| Extras       | (2 lb, 18 nb)            | 20  |
| Total        | (8 wkts, dec., 37.5 ovs) | 223 |

Fall of wickets:

1-10 (Pagon), 2-53 (Smith), 3-57 (Ganga), 4-108 (Morton), 5-157 (Bravo), 6-195 (Hinds), 7-215 (Hibbert), 8-223 (Black)

**Nottinghamshire bowling**

|  | Ovs | Ms | Runs | Wkts |
|---|---|---|---|---|
| Malik | 13 | 2 | 84 | 2 |
| Savill | 5 | 1 | 42 | 2 |
| Clough | 13 | 1 | 61 | 2 |
| Shafayat | 3 | 0 | 12 | 0 |
| McMahon | 3.5 | 0 | 22 | 2 |

**Nottinghamshire second innings**          **Runs**

| | | |
|---|---|---|
| GE Welton | not out | 8 |
| BM Shafayat | not out | 18 |
| V Atri | | |
| *+WM Noon | | |
| KP Pietersen | | |
| SR Patel | | |
| WR Smith | | |
| GD Clough | | |
| TE Savill | | |
| PJ McMahon | | |
| MN Malik | | |
| Extras | (1 b, 7 lb, 4 nb) | 12 |
| Total | (0 wkts, 7.4 overs) | 38 |

**West Indies A bowling**

|  | Ovs | Ms | Runs | Wkts |
|---|---|---|---|---|
| Black | 4 | 0 | 18 | 0 |
| Lawson | 3 | 0 | 12 | 0 |
| Best | 0.4 | 0 | 0 | 0 |

A similar fixture was arranged in 2006 with Sylvester Joseph, of Antigua, skippering the tourists, six of whom had already experienced Test cricket, plus Darren Sammy, who would go on to become West Indian captain in all three formats of the game.

Josh Mierkalns was given his Nottinghamshire debut, but it was another youngster, Mark Footitt, who would make the biggest impression on the opening day, taking 5-45. As with the previous match of its kind four years earlier, rain ruled out the prospect of a positive finish, with no play possible on the final day.

# Nottinghamshire v West Indies 'A'

Trent Bridge
16th, 17th, 18th August 2006 (3-day match)
Toss: won by West Indies A, who elected to bat
Umpires: NA Mallender, P Willey

## Result: Match drawn

### West Indies A first innings

| | | |
|---|---|---|
| DS Smith | c Smith b Clough | 51 |
| LMP Simmons | c Franks b Harris | 29 |
| *SC Joseph | lbw b Footitt | 26 |
| RS Morton | lbw b Footitt | 35 |
| DR Smith | lbw b Harris | 18 |
| +PA Browne | b Clough | 1 |
| DJG Sammy | b Footitt | 17 |
| DBL Powell | c Clough b Franks | 0 |
| RA Kelly | not out | 2 |
| D Mohammed | b Footitt | 2 |
| AP Richardson | lbw b Footitt | 4 |
| Extras | (7 lb, 4 nb, 15 w) | 26 |
| Total | (all out, 55 ovs) | 211 |

Fall of wickets:
1-51 (Simmons), 2-112 (Joseph), 3-126 (DS Smith), 4-169 (DR Smith), 5-170 (Browne), 6-179 (Morton), 7-180 (Powell), 8-200 (Sammy), 9-206 (Mohammed), 10-211 (Richardson)

## Nottinghamshire bowling

|          | Ovs | Ms | Runs | Wkts |
|----------|-----|----|------|------|
| Harris   | 15  | 4  | 52   | 2    |
| Franks   | 14  | 0  | 45   | 1    |
| Clough   | 13  | 4  | 56   | 2    |
| Footitt  | 12  | 1  | 45   | 5    |
| McMahon  | 1   | 0  | 6    | 0    |

## Nottinghamshire first innings

| | | |
|---|---|---|
| *JER Gallian | c Mohammed b Sammy | 50 |
| DJ Bicknell | c Browne b Powell | 44 |
| WR Smith | lbw b Sammy | 2 |
| SR Patel | not out | 66 |
| +D Alleyne | c Sammy b Powell | 2 |
| JA Mierkalns | c Simmons b Mohammed | 18 |
| PJ Franks | not out | 10 |
| GD Clough | | |
| PJ McMahon | | |
| MHA Footitt | | |
| AJ Harris | | |
| Extras | (7 nb, 6 w) | 13 |
| Total | (5 wkts, 70.2 ovs) | 205 |

Fall of wickets:1-73 (Gallian), 2-79 (Smith), 3-111 (Bicknell), 4-135 (Alleyne), 5-187 (Mierkalns

## West Indies A bowling

|            | Ovs | Ms | Runs | Wkts |
|------------|-----|----|------|------|
| Powell     | 14  | 5  | 31   | 2    |
| Richardson | 7.2 | 1  | 31   | 0    |
| Kelly      | 9   | 1  | 50   | 0    |
| Sammy      | 18  | 10 | 27   | 2    |
| DR Smith   | 16  | 7  | 60   | 0    |
| Mohammed   | 6   | 3  | 6    | 1    |

# Recent times

# 2007

Ramnaresh Sarwan, of Guyana, was given the captaincy of the West Indies for their 2007 tour of the British Isles, which included four Tests, two Twenty20 internationals and then three ODIs, the last of which was staged at Trent Bridge.

By the time they arrived in Nottingham the tourists could have been excused for being a little weary. They had taken a 3-0 beating in the Test series, with Sarwan's injury in the Second Test ruling him out for the rest of the tour, leaving his deputy, Daren Ganga, in charge for the final two Test matches. Chris Gayle took over for the shorter formats, with the Twenty20 series being split one-all and the first two ODIs also being shared.

With the outcome of the series depending on the result in Nottingham, Gayle won an important toss and decided to bat. Kevin Pietersen, once of Notts, and Stuart Broad, later to join the county, were both included in an England side led by Durham's Paul Collingwood. Gayle made 82 at the top of the order for his side, a score that was matched by Runako Morton, a powerful hitter from Nevis in the Leeward Islands, as West Indies posted an impressive 289-5.

Losing wickets early and regularly proved to be England's undoing, with Jamaica's Daren Powell dismissing Cook, Prior, Pietersen and Broad on the way to securing a convincing 93-run victory for his team.

# England v West Indies

Third One Day International
Trent Bridge, Nottingham
7th July, 2007
Toss: won by West Indies, who elected to bat
Umpires: MR Benson, BG Jerling

## Result: West Indies won by 93 runs

**West Indies innings**

| | | Runs | Balls | Mins | 4s | 6s | S-Rate |
|---|---|---|---|---|---|---|---|
| *CH Gayle | c and b Plunkett | 82 | 126 | 171 | 8 | - | 65.08 |
| DS Smith | c Bell b Anderson | 13 | 9 | 10 | 3 | - | 144.44 |
| S Chanderpaul | c Pietersen b Plunkett | 33 | 47 | 72 | 3 | 1 | 70.21 |
| MN Samuels | c Prior b Plunkett | 9 | 7 | 10 | 2 | - | 128.57 |
| RS Morton | not out | 82 | 89 | 115 | 6 | 1 | 92.13 |
| DJ Bravo | b Anderson | 42 | 24 | 38 | 6 | - | 175.00 |
| DR Smith | not out | 4 | 1 | 2 | 1 | - | 400.00 |
| +D Ramdin | | | | | | | |
| DBL Powell | | | | | | | |
| R Rampaul | | | | | | | |
| FH Edwards | | | | | | | |
| Extras | (5 b, 6 lb, 4 nb, 9 w) | 24 | | | | | |
| Total | (5 wkts, 50 ovs) | 289 | | | | | |

Fall of wickets:
1-16 (DS Smith, 2.3 ov), 2-93 (Chanderpaul, 20.1 ov), 3-108 (Samuels, 22.4 ov), 4-193 (Gayle, 41.6 ov), 5-285 (Bravo, 49.5 ov)

**England bowling**

| | Ovs | Ms | Runs | Wkts | Ws | NBs | S-Rate | Econ |
|---|---|---|---|---|---|---|---|---|
| Anderson | 10 | 0 | 51 | 2 | 1 | 1 | 30.00 | 5.10 |
| Plunkett | 10 | 0 | 59 | 3 | 4 | 1 | 20.00 | 5.90 |
| Broad | 9 | 0 | 71 | 0 | 3 | 1 | - | 7.89 |

| | | | | | | | | |
|---|---|---|---|---|---|---|---|---|
| Panesar | 6 | 0 | 28 | 0 | - | - | - | 4.67 |
| Mascarenhas | 8 | 0 | 28 | 0 | - | - | - | 3.50 |
| Collingwood | 7 | 0 | 41 | 0 | - | - | - | 5.86 |

## England innings

| | | Runs | Balls | Mins | 4s | 6s | S-Rate |
|---|---|---|---|---|---|---|---|
| AN Cook | c DR Smith b Powell | 18 | 27 | 35 | 4 | - | 66.67 |
| +MJ Prior | c Ramdin b Powell | 1 | 5 | 9 | - | - | 20.00 |
| IR Bell | c DR Smith b Edwards | 27 | 45 | 68 | 4 | - | 60.00 |
| KP Pietersen | c DS Smith b Powell | 0 | 2 | 1 | - | - | 0.00 |
| OA Shah | c Ramdin b DR Smith | 51 | 66 | 86 | 4 | 1 | 77.27 |
| *PD Collingwood | b Bravo | 44 | 50 | 61 | 3 | - | 88.00 |
| AD Mascarenhas | c Gayle b Edwards | 5 | 12 | 18 | - | - | 41.67 |
| LE Plunkett | c Samuels b Edwards | 2 | 7 | 14 | - | - | 28.57 |
| SCJ Broad | c Gayle b Powell | 5 | 15 | 17 | - | - | 33.33 |
| MS Panesar | lbw b Rampaul | 13 | 24 | 31 | 2 | - | 54.17 |
| JM Anderson | not out | 11 | 17 | 24 | - | - | 64.71 |
| Extras | (4 b, 3 lb, 4 nb, 8 w) | 19 | | | | | |
| Total | (all out, 44.2 ovs) | 196 | | | | | |

Fall of wickets:
1-6 (Prior, 2.2 ov), 2-29 (Cook, 8.3 ov), 3-33 (Pietersen, 8.5 ov), 4-72 (Bell, 17.6 ov), 5-144 (Shah, 30.4 ov), 6-162 (Collingwood, 33.5 ov), 7-162 (Mascarenhas, 34.1 ov), 8-168 (Plunkett, 36.3 ov), 9-171 (Broad, 37.5 ov), 10-196 (Panesar, 44.2 ov)

## West Indies bowling

| | Ovs | Ms | Runs | Wkts | Ws | NBs | S-Rate | Econ |
|---|---|---|---|---|---|---|---|---|
| Powell | 10 | 2 | 40 | 4 | - | - | 15.00 | 4.00 |
| Rampaul | 7.2 | 0 | 25 | 1 | 3 | - | 44.00 | 3.41 |
| DR Smith | 10 | 0 | 60 | 1 | 2 | - | 60.00 | 6.00 |
| Edwards | 10 | 1 | 30 | 3 | 2 | 2 | 20.00 | 3.00 |
| Gayle | 2 | 0 | 11 | 0 | - | - | - | 5.50 |
| Bravo | 5 | 0 | 23 | 1 | 1 | 2 | 30.00 | 4.60 |

# 2009

During the ICC World Twenty20 tournament in 2009, West Indies played a Group match against Sri Lanka at Trent Bridge. Tillekeratne Dilshan and Sanath Jayasuriya, two of the most formidable batsmen around in the shortest format of the game, gave Sri Lanka a flying start before they were parted in the 13th over with 124 on the board.

Both players fell to Lendl Simmons, Dilshan for 74 and his partner for 81, with the same bowler then getting rid of Sangakarra and Jayawardena in quick succession also, to end with figures of 4-19 from just three overs.

Chasing 193 for victory, West Indies struggled against a strong attack and, despite Dwayne Bravo's 51, they fell 15 runs short, thereby losing only their second ever game at Trent Bridge.

# Sri Lanka v West Indies

ICC World Twenty20 (Group C)
Trent Bridge, Nottingham
10 June 2009
Toss: won by West Indies who decided to field
Umpires: BF Bowden, SJA Taufel

## Result: Sri Lanka won by 15 runs

**Sri Lanka innings**

|  |  | Runs | Balls | Mins | 4s | 6s | S-Rate |
|---|---|---|---|---|---|---|---|
| TM Dilshan | c Benn b Simmons | 74 | 47 | 82 | 11 | 1 | 157.45 |
| ST Jayasuriya | lbw b Simmons | 81 | 47 | 55 | 10 | 3 | 172.34 |
| *+KC Sangakkara | c Fletcher b Simmons | 5 | 6 | 9 | - | - | 83.33 |
| DPMD Jayawardene | c Ramdin b Simmons | 4 | 7 | 11 | - | - | 57.14 |
| J Mubarak | not out | 8 | 5 | 13 | 1 | - | 160.00 |
| LPC Silva | c Ramdin b Taylor | 7 | 7 | 7 | 1 | - | 100.00 |
| AD Mathews | not out | 3 | 2 | 1 | - | - | 150.00 |
| BAW Mendis |  |  |  |  |  |  |  |
| I Udana |  |  |  |  |  |  |  |
| M Muralitharan |  |  |  |  |  |  |  |
| SL Malinga |  |  |  |  |  |  |  |
| Extras | (5 lb, 1 nb, 4 w) | 10 |  |  |  |  |  |
| Total | (5 wkts., 20 ovs) | 192 |  |  |  |  |  |

Fall of wickets:
1-124 (Jayasuriya, 12.3 ov), 2-147 (Sangakkara, 14.5 ov), 3-168 (Jayawardene, 17.2 ov), 4-172 (Dilshan, 17.4 ov), 5-189 (Silva, 19.4 ov)

**West Indies bowling**

|  | Ovs | Ms | Runs | Wkts | Ws | NBs | S-Rate | Econ |
|---|---|---|---|---|---|---|---|---|
| Taylor | 4 | 0 | 32 | 1 | - | 1 | 24.00 | 8.00 |
| Edwards | 2 | 0 | 37 | 0 | - | - | - | 18.50 |
| Bravo | 4 | 0 | 29 | 0 | 3 | - | - | 7.25 |
| Benn | 4 | 0 | 25 | 0 | - | - | - | 6.25 |

| | | | | | | | | | |
|---|---|---|---|---|---|---|---|---|---|
| Pollard | 3 | 0 | 45 | 0 | I | - | - | 15.00 |
| Simmons | 3 | 0 | 19 | 4 | - | - | 4.50 | 6.33 |

## West Indies innings

| | | Runs | Balls | Mins | 4s | 6s | S-Rate |
|---|---|---|---|---|---|---|---|
| LMP Simmons | c Jayawardene b Murali | 29 | 19 | 29 | 5 | - | 152.63 |
| ADS Fletcher | b Malinga | 13 | 11 | 12 | I | I | 118.18 |
| XM Marshall | c Silva b Mendis | 14 | 11 | 16 | I | - | 127.27 |
| S Chanderpaul | b Mendis | I | 5 | 5 | - | - | 20.00 |
| RR Sarwan | not out | 28 | 26 | 58 | - | - | 107.69 |
| DJ Bravo | c Mubarak b Malinga | 51 | 38 | 38 | 5 | 2 | 134.21 |
| KA Pollard | not out | 19 | 11 | 16 | 3 | - | 172.73 |
| *+D Ramdin | | | | | | | |
| SJ Benn | | | | | | | |
| JE Taylor | | | | | | | |
| FH Edwards | | | | | | | |
| Extras | (4 lb, I nb, 17 w) | 22 | | | | | |
| Total | (5 wkts., 20 ovs) | 177 | | | | | |

Fall of wickets:

1-38 (Fletcher, 3.2 ov), 2-70 (Simmons, 6.4 ov), 3-71 (Marshall, 7.1 ov), 4-73 (Chanderpaul, 7.5 ov), 5-150 (Bravo, 17.3 ov)

## Sri Lanka bowling

| | Ovs | Ms | Runs | Wkts | Ws | NBs | S-Rate | Econ |
|---|---|---|---|---|---|---|---|---|
| Jayasuriya | 3 | 0 | 34 | 0 | I | - | - | 11.33 |
| Malinga | 4 | 0 | 45 | 2 | 2 | - | 12.00 | 11.25 |
| Udana | 4 | 0 | 36 | 0 | 5 | - | - | 9.00 |
| Mendis | 4 | 0 | 25 | 2 | - | - | 12.00 | 6.25 |
| Muralitharan | 4 | 0 | 21 | I | I | - | 24.00 | 5.25 |
| Mathews | I | 0 | 12 | 0 | - | I | - | 12.00 |

# DARREN BRAVO

### *Date of birth: 6 February 1989 Santa Cruz, Trinidad*

With neither David Hussey or Adam Voges available for the final four matches of the 2011 LV= County Championship programme, Notts' director of cricket, Mick Newell, scoured the planet for someone capable of bolstering his sometimes fragile top order. His sights eventually fell upon a 22-year-old left hander from Trinidad and Tobago, Darren Bravo, who had already played international cricket in all three disciplines, Test, ODI and T20.

Bravo had played just two matches in England before – during a West Indies A tour the previous year. His Trent Bridge debut produced a score of 25 in a rain-interrupted Clydesdale Bank 40 victory over Glamorgan.

Darren, younger half-brother of fellow international Dwayne Bravo, and cousin of Brian Lara, quickly adjusted to life on the county circuit and turned in several useful performances during his brief introduction to our domestic game.

In seven first class innings he averaged 35, with a top score of 70 coming at Edgbaston against Warwickshire. He also scored 53 against Sussex and a one day 62 against Lancashire

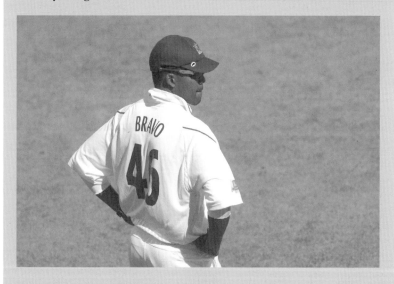

# Barbados 2012

As preparation for the impending county season in England, Nottinghamshire's cricketers undertook their first official tour to Barbados in March 2012. Along with five other counties, the Notts boys took part in a well-orchestrated series of fixtures in all three disciplines, 40-over, Twenty20 cricket and a two-day match in traditional white clothing with a red ball.

The tour party was: Mick Newell (director of cricket), Wayne Noon (coach), Kevin Paxton (fitness coach), Ross Hollinworth (physio), Chris Read (captain), Paul Franks, Alex Hales, Neil Edwards, Michael Lumb, James Taylor, Karl Turner, Riki Wessels, Scott Elstone, Steven Mullaney, Graeme White, Ben Phillips, Luke Fletcher, Andrew Carter, Harry Gurney, Jake Ball and George Bacon.

The players didn't have long to get over their flight, being quickly sent out on to the training ground to acclimatise themselves. Former Nottinghamshire all-rounder Franklyn Stephenson had recently opened a new facility, close to the players' resort, and he was happy that his former county side became the first professional team to train at the centre.

Throughout the tour Notts practiced at Franklyn's academy, with the host usually in attendance to add support and words of wisdom. Stephenson, a former Trent Bridge team-mate of Mick Newell's, had become a golf professional towards the end of his own cricketing days and has remained as the club pro at the exclusive Sandy Lane course ever since.

"I made the decision towards the end of my cricketing career," he explained. "There weren't any golf professionals in Barbados at the time and I helped set up the Professional Golfers' Association here. It's actually saved me a fortune in green fees around the world!

After a tough first session, Mick Newell praised Franklyn's new academy. "I think it's excellent," he said. "The pitches and the outfield are good and we've had four strips properly prepared

for us to practice on and we're looking to make the most of the opportunity to train here."

Back in 1988 Stephenson became only the second man after Richard Hadlee, also with Nottinghamshire four years earlier, to complete the double, a feat he is understandably proud of. "It was my first season with Notts," he said. "I'd come in as the overseas professional to replace Rice and Hadlee and all I wanted to do was give them a reason to remember me by – I hope I did that!"

Surveying his former county practicing for the first time in his homeland, he seemed quite emotional. "To have Notts here is, literally, a dream come true for me."

Notts Outlaws were defeated in the opening match of their Barbados tour, losing to Warwickshire Bears by just 14 runs. Chasing a victory target of 207, the Outlaws were dismissed for 192 with just seven balls of the innings remaining.

Mick Newell described this as a typical pre-season friendly, with no batsman on either side reaching fifty. Notts fell short in their victory chase, despite having three players, Franks, Wessels and Elstone, getting into the 30s but falling when well-set.

*Sat 17 March 2012 40-over match v Warwickshire*
*Windward CC*
*Warwickshire 206-7 Maddy 45, Elstone 2-17*
*Nottinghamshire 192 Franks 32, Carter 3-28*
*Warwickshire won by 14 runs*

Nottinghamshire's cricketers received a very pleasant surprise at a 'Welcome Meeting' staged to greet them and the five other first-class county sides that were out enjoying the facilities in Barbados. Fashionably late and totally unexpected, Sir Garfield Sobers arrived at the function in Limegrove at Holetown.

A warm and spontaneous round of applause broke out as Sir Garfield, now 75, explained that his good friend Franklyn Stephenson had telephoned to see if he would be able to come and meet the county's current players. Sobers, considered to be the greatest all-rounder of them all, with 8,035 runs and 235 wickets in Test cricket, played for Nottinghamshire between 1968 and 1974.

Seen as one of the unfashionable clubs at the time, Sobers did much to change the image of his new county and recalled fondly some of the characters he shared a dressing room with. "We had some good cricketers there at that time. Mike Harris really should have played for England in 1971 when he scored nine centuries in the season, and so should Barry Stead."

Stead, a whole-hearted Yorkshireman who died in 1980, took 98 first-class wickets in 1972. "He gave everything that year, yet England continued to overlook him. We had good players like Basher Hassan and Mike Smedley – and then Derek Randall got into the team. I said after just one season that he would play Test cricket – and he did."

Sir Garfield wished his old county side the very best of fortunes in the forthcoming knock-out competition, the Banks Barbados T20 Cup, as well as in the new domestic campaign back home. He then spent time chatting to director of cricket Mick Newell, captain Chris Read and his side.

Newell admitted that the visit had turned a good evening into a memorable one. "It was terrific of him to come and see the players and spend time with them," said Newell. "He has been happy to have his photograph taken with them all and chat to them about their careers."

England Twenty20 international Alex Hales admitted that Sir Garfield's visit had meant a lot to the team. "It's great to meet someone like that," he said. "We all know what a fantastic cricketer he was and for him to come and wish us well has been a big thing for the lads."

An aggressive innings of 94 from opener Neil Edwards, backed up by 64 from Riki Wessels, paved the way for Notts Outlaws to complete a 64-run victory over Yorkshire at Pickwick Cricket Club, Barbados. Put in to bat, the Outlaws made a healthy 275-6 from their 40 overs and then bowled Yorkshire out for just 211.

A punishing innings of 94 by Neil Edwards was the decisive factor in the Outlaws first success of the tour. The left-hander scored his runs from just 91 deliveries faced, with five 4s and six 6s, four of them in quick succession off Rashid. Riki Wessels' innings of 64 was ended by an outrageous piece of athleticism on the boundary by Adam Lyth.

*Mon 19 March 2012 40-over match v Yorkshire*
*Four Square Oval*
*Nottinghamshire 275-6 Edwards 94, Wessels 64*
*Yorkshire 211 Sayers 65, Fletcher 3-29*
*Nottinghamshire won by 64 runs*

The Outlaws advanced to the semi finals of The Banks Barbados T20 Cup with a thoroughly professional four-wicket win over the island side at Kensington Oval. Batting first after winning the toss, Barbados made 130-4, with Ben Phillips taking 3-25. Always ahead of the rate, the Outlaws reached their victory target for the loss of six wickets with eleven balls to spare.

*Wed 21 March 2012 Twenty20 match v Barbados*
*The Banks Barbados T20 Cup Quarter-Final*
*Kensington Oval, Bridgetown*
*Barbados 130-4 Mayers 37, Phillips 3-25*
*Nottinghamshire 134-6 Lumb 44, Smith 3-20*
*Nottinghamshire win by 4 wickets*

Amongst the opposition ranks was a former Nottinghamshire favourite. Vasbert Drakes, who played for the county in 1999, is now making his way as a member of the backroom staff at Kensington Oval, as he explained during the evening.

"I'm part of the coaching set-up here at Kensington now and am principally responsible for the bowling department within the BCA (Barbados Cricket Association).

"I've got many happy memories of my season with Nottinghamshire. I was certainly happy with how things went for me that year, with 80 first class wickets and another 27 in the one-day matches. I think only

Somerset's Andy Caddick took more that season. Trent Bridge was a happy hunting ground for me, particularly bowling down the hill because it seemed to swing a little bit."

Drakes is perhaps best remembered for his astonishing feat of taking four wickets in four balls against Derbyshire in a CGU National League match, turning an inevitable defeat into an unbelievable victory. "Obviously that's not something that you do every day, so it remains a special moment in my career The game was definitely slipping away for us, so to do that in the last over was very, very enjoyable."

Vasbert remains friends with some of his former team-mates. "I try and keep in touch with guys like Paul Franks, Chris Read and Chris Cairns. Obviously, I don't see them as often as I can as we are all busy travelling the world, but it's nice to catch up and it's always a pleasure to go back to Trent Bridge whenever I can."

Notts Outlaws bowed out of The Banks Barbados T20 Cup after losing to Yorkshire by 38 runs at a very hot Windward Cricket Club. Captain Andrew Gale was the man who hurt the Outlaws, scoring a punishing 111 (63 balls, 82 mins, 13x4s 3x6s) out of a total of 192-4.

In response Notts could only make 154, being bowled out with the final ball of the eighteenth over. Neil Edwards top-scored for the Outlaws, with 59, but his dismissal signalled the end of any realistic challenge.

*Thur 22 March 2012 Twenty20 match v Yorkshire*
*The Banks Barbados T20 Cup Semi-Final*
*Windward CC*
*Yorkshire 192-4 Gale 111*
*Nottinghamshire 154 Edwards 59, Rashid 3-31*
*Yorkshire won by 38 runs*

Half-centuries from Chris Read, Steven Mullaney and Alex Hales lifted Nottinghamshire to 279-5 declared on the first day of their two-day match against Warwickshire at Windward CC. Pre-determined to bat for 60 overs, Notts then spent a session in the field during which the Bears posted 96-4 from 30 overs.

The final day's cricket of the tour saw a continuation of the two-day match with a reversal of the first day, with Warwickshire batting first for 60 overs. They made 148-7, with Notts replying with 127-2. On the bowling front Graeme White's left-arm spin brought him three wickets, with Neil Edwards again looking composed at the crease, making a classy 60 before retiring.

*Sat 24 and Sun 25 March 2012 Two-day Friendly v Warwickshire*
*Windward CC*
*Nottinghamshire 279-5 dec Read 82, Mullaney 76 not out, Hales*
*60, Barker 2-27 & 127-2 Edwards 60 ret, Carter 2-26*
*Warwickshire 96-4 dec & 148-7 Maddy 31, White 3-26*
*Match Drawn*

There was even a 'cricket-theme' on Nottinghamshire's return flight home. Ricardo Ellcock, the former Worcestershire and Middlesex pace bowler, who went on one England tour before retiring from the game to become an airline pilot was the captain on the player's returning Virgin Atlantic flight.

# STATISTICS

## ENGLAND V WEST INDIES TEST MATCHES AT TRENT BRIDGE

Test Matches Played:                        8
Test Matches Won by West Indies:            4
Test Matches Won by England:                0
Test Matches Drawn:                         4

### Test Match Records for West Indies at Trent Bridge

Highest Team Score:           558 in 1950
Lowest Team Score:            235 in 1966

Highest Individual Score:     261 FM Worrell 1950

Other Centuries:

| | | |
|---|---|---|
| 232 IVA Richards | 1976 |
| 209 B F Butcher | 1966 |
| 191* FM Worrell | 1957 |
| 168 OG Smith | 1957 |
| 152 BC Lara | 1995 |
| 129 ED Weekes | 1950 |

Best Bowling Performances

| | |
|---|---|
| 6-69 MD Marshall | 1988 |
| 5-69 KCG Benjamin | 1995 (2$^{nd}$ inns) |
| 5-72 AME Roberts | 1980 |
| 5-74 CEL Ambrose | 1991 |
| 5-105 KCG Benjamin | 1995 (1$^{st}$ inns) |
| 5-135 S Ramadhin | 1950 |

Highest Partnerships For Each Wicket:

| | | |
|---|---|---|
| 1st 103* AF Rae & JB Stollmeyer | | 1950 |
| 2nd 140 SL Campbell & BC Lara | | 1995 |
| 3rd 303 IVA Richards and AI Kallicharran | | 1976 |
| 4th 283 FMM Worrell and ED Weekes | | 1950 |
| 5th 173 GS Sobers & BF Butcher | | 1966 |
| 6th 105 OG Smith & DS Atkinson | | 1957 |
| 7th 154 OG Smith & JDC Goddard | | 1957 |
| 8th 91 MD Marshall & CEL Ambrose | | 1988 |
| 9th 34 MD Marshall & CA Walsh | | 1991 |
| 10th 55 FMM Worrell & S Ramadhin | | 1957 |

## Test Match Records for England versus West Indies at Trent Bridge

Highest Team Score:      619-6 dec in 1957
Lowest Team Score:      211 in 1991

Highest Individual Score:  258 TW Graveney 1957

Other centuries:

| | |
|---|---|
| 146 GA Gooch | 1988 |
| 126 PE Richardson | 1957 |
| 118* GA Hick | 1995 |
| 113 MA Atherton | 1995 |
| 109 T W Graveney | 1966 |
| 106 DS Steele | 1976 |
| 104 PBH May | 1957 |
| 102 C Washbrook | 1950 |

Best Bowling Performances:

| | |
|---|---|
| 5-63 FS Trueman | 1957 |
| 5-65 RGD Willis | 1980 |
| 5-118 JB Statham | 1957 |
| 5-127 AV Bedser | 1950 |

Highest Partnerships For Each Wicket:

1st 212 C Washbrook & RT Simpson          1950
2nd 266 PE Richardson & TW Graveney       1957
3rd 207 TW Graveney & PBH May             1957
4th 169 TW Graveney & MC Cowdrey          1966
5th 63 MC Cowdrey & DW Richardson         1957
6th 84 GA Hick & RC Russell               1995
7th 57 GA Hick & M Watkinson              1995
8th 60 GA Hick & DG Cork                  1995
9th 42 RA Smith & RK Illingworth          1991
10th 65 BL D'Oliveira & DL Underwood      1966


# West Indies at Trent Bridge – other matches:

Other First Class Matches Played    14
Other First Class Matches Won        4
Other First Class Matches Drawn     10
Other First Class Matches Lost       0
One Day Internationals Played        5
One Day Internationals Won           4
One Day Internationals Lost          1
Twenty20 Matches Played              1
Twenty20 Matches Lost                1

# AUTOGRAPHS